Essential 3ds Max® 8

Josh Robinson

Wordware Publishing, Inc.

Library of Congress Cataloging-in-Publication Data

Robinson, Josh.
Essential 3DS max 8 / by Josh Robinson.
   p. cm.
   Includes index.
   ISBN-13: 978-1-55622-485-0 (pbk.)
   ISBN-10: 1-55622-485-0 (pbk.)
   1. Computer animation. 2. 3ds max (Computer file). 3. Computer graphics.
   I. Title.
   TR897.7.R63 2006
   006.6'96--dc22   2006006512

ISBN-13: 978-1-55622-485-0
ISBN-10: 1-55622-485-0

10 9 8 7 6 5 4 3 2 1
0603

All inquiries for volume purchases of this book should be addressed to Wordware Publishing, Inc., at the above address. Telephone inquiries may be made by calling:

(972) 423-0090

Dedication

To both of my parents. Had they not had the foresight and open-mindedness to believe in me and what I wanted to do even when I was very young, I would have gone to the same community college as everyone else and completely wasted any potential talent and opportunity. I am now a 3D artist living in Santa Monica and enjoy my life to the absolute fullest. They gave me this life simply by believing in me and trusting that I would make the most of the opportunity they were providing.

Contents

Introduction

Hello, fellow 3D enthusiasts! First, I want to say thank you very much for picking up *Essential 3ds Max 8*. I hope this book will answer all or most of the questions you have run into while using 3D Studio MAX. With a little luck, I will even inspire you a bit.

In this book, we will touch on all the major aspects of 3D Studio MAX — everything from customizing the user interface to creating a composite shot with your own background plate. I really tried to go out of my way to fill the book with quality art that would inspire other 3D artists, while trying not to overwhelm them with unattainable goals. Often I pick up these types of books and, although I find them informative, find the quality of the work inside to be a bit uninspired. I mean, who wants to model a doorknob? It's less than exciting, to say the least. They also always seem to leave out the things that absolutely every beginner wants to know, like How do you model an ear? How can I get better at modeling characters? What are some common industry mistakes? We will discuss all these things in great detail in this book.

By the time you are done with this book, not only will you be a 3D Jedi, but money will literally fall from the sky. Also note that you will most likely be signing autographs all the time. You may even need to hire a personal bodyguard to keep your newfound fans at bay. Well, not quite. But you can accomplish anything you set your mind to. If anything, I hope this book inspires you. Maybe you'll learn a small technique or see a character that you want to model. Either way, I hope it inspires you to keep moving forward. Keep learning and never quit. You can accomplish anything in life.

✎ **Note:**

The companion files are available for download at www.wordware.com/files/3dsmax. The files include color images of all the figures in the book and example files used in the modeling chapters.

Chapter 1

Understanding 3D Space

I was very young when my mother put me in our ugly silver Cutlass and drove me to the movies. I was very excited. I was going to see a little movie called *Jurassic Park*. I sat there eating my popcorn and sipping a Coke that was much too large for me. Then something unbelievable happened. I saw a T. rex running after an SUV filled with people! It was the very moment that I knew what I wanted to do for a living. I had never seen anything like that. It was so real. It was as if you could just reach through the screen and touch it. Film was never the same after *Jurassic Park*. The movie set a standard and raised the bar above anything else we had seen up to that point.

What Exactly Is 3D Space and How Does It Work?

When you break down the T. rex and strip away all his skin, muscle, animation, and claws, you are left with a model that is made up of a series of points in 3D space. It's like a very complex game of connect-the-dots. Everything in 3D space is driven by the things I tried to avoid in school: math and geometry. Thankfully, everything happens in the background. Many people think you have to be a programmer or good at math to be a 3D artist. This is *not* true. In fact, I'm still quite sure that 4 + 4 = 239.

When using 3D software, space is calculated by defining where something is in that space. Everything is given three coordinates: an X position, a Y position, and a Z position. Left and right is X, toward and away is Y, up and down is Z. Everything you ever create in 3D will have its own XYZ coordinate.

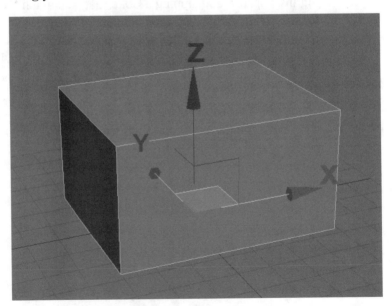

Figure 1-1: 3D space coordinates.

The box in Figure 1-1, for example, has a position in 3D space. To me (the artist), it's just a box and I can move it around at will. I may want to move it left a little bit or right a little bit, but I don't often have to concern myself with an object's exact position. 3D Studio MAX does this for me because Max knows its exact point in 3D space. All this is done on the fly and isn't something you really need to concern yourself with in the beginning. Eventually, when you are a 3D Jedi, you may care that something is exactly –345.8475 on the X axis, but until then you can just relax.

Basic 3D Objects (Standard Primitives)

Almost everything you create in 3ds Max will be based on a simple object. No matter how complex the render or how detailed the model, it's always a simple object at its core.

Take the following, for example.

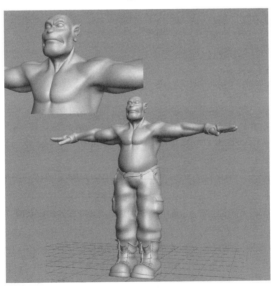

Figure 1-2

As complicated as it is, at its core it is still a wireframe that can be created by starting off with a simple box.

3D Studio MAX gives you a host of objects to start off with called standard primitives. These objects are located inside the Create panel under the geometry section.

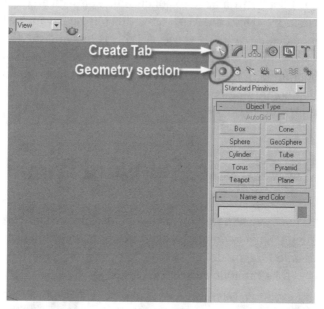

Figure 1-3: You must be in the Create panel to access the Geometry tab.

 Note:

The Create panel has several sub-tabs: Geometry, Shapes, Lights, Cameras, Helpers, and so on. We will be visiting these other areas later in the book as we learn.

These are the basic 3D objects that you will see in most 3D packages. (Unless you are using Maya and you need a tube, which they still don't provide for some reason. But I digress...) Anyway, the basic standard primitives are: box, sphere, tube, torus, cylinder, pyramid, cone, geosphere, and plane, which are available as buttons in the Object Type list.

Max has also taken it a step further and given you even more objects in the Extended Primitives drop-down. You can access these extended primitives by pressing the drop-down arrow next to Standard Primitives.

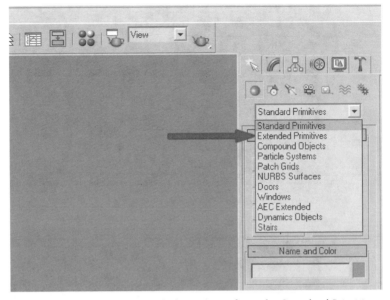

Figure 1-4: Access the extended primitives from the Standard Primitives drop-down.

This list gives you even more objects with more options. In most cases, these will be very helpful for industrial or machinery design. These are things that although simple are mind-numbingly tedious to create in large quantities. I am personally grateful for these extra primitives. 3D Studio MAX even gives you primitives for stairs, windows, and doors.

Figure 1-5: Stairs primitives.

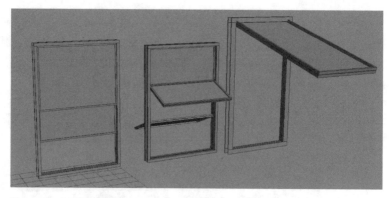

Figure 1-6: Windows primitives.

Figure 1-7: Doors primitives.

These primitives are located in the Standard Primitives drop-down, and they act just like the other primitives in that you have sliders that will affect height, width, depth, etc. You can even change the way the windows and doors open. You can make them double doors or windows, and so on. The pivots are created and adjusted on the fly so that everything opens and closes on the proper hinge. This is an extremely fast way to create simple things that would ordinarily take a

Figure 1-8: Access the Doors, Windows, and Stairs primitives options in the Standard Primitives drop-down.

bit of time. From my experience in working in architecture for many years, I can't tell you how much easier it is to generate a spiral staircase exactly to spec on the fly, compared to doing all the math and modeling and unwrapping that would otherwise have been involved.

Likewise, Max gives you a few other treats such as the ability to create trees and walls on the fly. These are located in the AEC Extended section of the drop-down.

Figure 1-9: Choose AEC Extended from the Standard Primitives drop-down to find additional objects.

These are pretty neat additions to the Max arsenal. Figure 1-10 shows just a few examples of the procedural trees that Max can create for you.

Figure 1-10: Standard trees.

Lights

Lights play an important role when creating anything in 3D. In fact, without proper lighting it doesn't matter what you make or how good you make it; if it's not lit properly, your 3D object can look as flat and boring as a sheet of paper. Lighting is what gives everything depth. You only know that a ball is round because of the way light bounces off it, as shown in Figure 1-11.

If you flooded that same ball with light from all directions, it would be just as flat as a sheet of paper (see Figure 1-12).

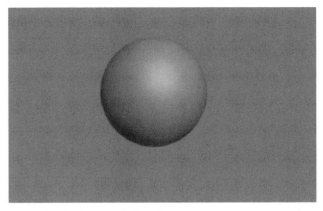

Figure 1-11: A properly lit sphere.

Figure 1-12: A sphere that looks flat because it is overlit.

Certain lights will accomplish certain things for you. Knowing how to properly use your lights and having a good understanding of how light reacts in the real world will be invaluable to you as a 3D artist. The biggest misconception about lighting in 3D is that you simply add "lights" and Blam! — you are done with your lighting. This is not true. In fact, in most cases you are often faking real lighting in order to make your scene look realistic. What makes things look real is the way light bounces off objects. For example, when you stand outside and face the sun, your back will also be lit. Why is this? Because the sunlight is bouncing off the ground behind you and then back up to your legs, shoulders, head, etc. You can do this on the computer at the expense of severe render times, or you can fake it by using multiple lights. In the beginning, I think it is best to learn how to light without relying on the computer to do everything for you. After you learn how to light and create well-lit scenes on your own, then you can explore things like radiosity solutions, global illumination, and other renderers in order to create completely photo-realistic lighting.

Cameras

The camera is just what you think it is: a virtual camera that gives you something tangible to view and control in 3D space. When you are modeling and twirling around in 3ds Max you are actually looking through your Perspective viewport. The Perspective view is not something you can literally move and control. You can only *look* through it. A camera is actually something that you can see in your scene. You can view through your Max camera just like a home video camera. You can animate the camera, tell the camera to follow other objects, change the field of view (or your viewing angle), and so on.

When you are watching *The Lord of the Rings* and they take a camera from the top of a tower and then fly deep into the ground, it is because they created the set and then animated their virtual camera in that scene according to their desired camera path. Being able to create these CG environments and then animate a virtual camera through your environment is something that has completely changed filmmaking. There is no way to create the same shots in the movie *Spider-Man* with an actual camera. It is simply impossible to do it otherwise.

As you progress as a 3D artist you'll use cameras to create dramatic effects and make spectacular camera moves. Before you get to that point, however, you need to understand the user interface of 3D Studio MAX.

Chapter 2

3D Studio MAX at a Glance

Viewports and Basic Navigation

Well, here it is — 3D Studio MAX in all its glory.

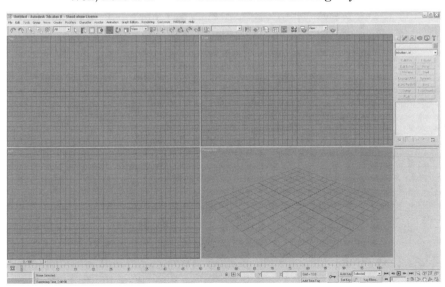

Figure 2-1: The standard view with four viewports.

Before we have you recreating scenes from *The Lord of the Rings* or anything too dramatic, you need to understand how the viewports work and how to properly navigate them. When you first load up 3D Studio MAX you will notice that your screen is broken up into quads. These are the four basic viewports (Top, Front, Left, and Perspective). This is the standard layout in most 3D packages. The only actual 3D viewport is your Perspective view. All others are two-dimensional views only.

If you look to the bottom-right corner of 3D Studio MAX you'll find the viewport navigation tools.

Figure 2-2: The viewport navigation tools.

These are the tools that will allow you to zoom in, zoom out, pan left and right, as well as rotate around your objects in the four views. There are two ways to zoom in 3ds Max. You can use the Zoom tool (identified by the magnifying glass), or you can use your mouse wheel to quickly zoom in and out.

Figure 2-3: The Zoom tool.

If you move your cursor to the Perspective viewport and left-click, you'll notice that it is highlighted by a yellow border. That means the Perspective viewport is now active. When the Perspective viewport is activated you can use your mouse wheel to zoom in and out. Rolling up will zoom in and rolling back will zoom out. If you want to use the Zoom tool, then just left-click the magnifying glass. Next, bring your cursor into the viewport, and hold the left-click down while dragging toward and away. You'll notice that you are now zooming in and out. These functions will work in any of the four viewports inside 3D Studio MAX.

There will be many times when you want to see something as large as possible and zooming in is just not enough. You may want to maximize your viewport so that you are only looking at a desired quad. To maximize the Perspective viewport, you must first make sure it is highlighted (as indicated by the yellow border). Next, select the Maximize Viewport toggle tool.

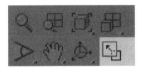

Figure 2-4: The Maximize Viewport tool.

When you select the Maximize Viewport tool you'll notice that your Perspective viewport now takes up the entire viewing area of 3D Studio MAX.

 Note:

The Maximize Viewport tool is a toggle button. If you want to minimize the viewport, simply hit the button again. The default hotkey for this function in Max is "W."

Now that you can zoom in and out and maximize your view, you need to know how to pan left and right within a view. Return to the navigation panel on the bottom right and select the Pan View tool (identified by the hand).

Figure 2-5: The Pan View tool.

Select the Pan View tool, then return to your Perspective viewport, hold the left-click on your mouse, and move the mouse around. You'll notice now that you can grab the entire view and move it up, down, left, and right. You can also achieve this by pressing and holding the mouse wheel down while moving the mouse.

Note:

Try to get comfortable using the mouse wheel for zooming and panning; it will speed up your workflow dramatically.

Now for the FUN stuff — rotating around your Perspective view! Go to your Perspective viewport and maximize it if necessary. Then go back to the viewport navigation tools on the bottom right and select the Rotate View tool.

Figure 2-6: The Rotate View tool.

This tool works the same as the others. After you select the Rotate View tool, go back to your Perspective viewport, hold the left-click, and start moving your mouse. You will be able to tell you're rotating around your view because the grid in the viewport will be moving.

Note:

When you are in Rotate View mode inside 3D Studio MAX, a circle will appear within the Perspective viewport. If you rotate within that circle, you will rotate around your scene. If you rotate outside of that circle, it rotates the entire view, similar to what would happen if you turned a camera on its side.

After you are comfortable with rotating around in your view, try using combinations of moves. Rotate around for a second and then pan to the right. Then zoom in and out. Then rotate your view again. Becoming quick at navigating your scene is something that will come with time. You do have to make an effort, however. Try to use the mouse wheel as often as possible instead of manually going to the viewport navigation tools every time you want to change functions. You will also find in time that you want to create hotkeys for some of these functions in order to improve your workflow.

The last tool I want to show you is the Zoom Extents tool.

Figure 2-7: The Zoom Extents tool.

Zoom extents is just a fancy way of saying that you want to bring the selected object or scene back into view. Sometimes you realize you have moved, panned, and rotated all over the place and your view is all turned around. Or maybe you simply want to select an object and then have Max zoom in on it for you. Just use Zoom Extents to perform that function. No object needs to be selected for this to work (which is good since we have not yet created anything).

Changing Viewport Windows

Depending on what you are doing, you may want to adjust
your viewports in 3D Studio MAX. There are many ways to do
this; the most basic way is to just manually move them to suit
your needs. For example, I want to see all four views but make
the Perspective viewport larger. When you left-click and hold
one of the viewport's border lines, you will notice that your
cursor changes to a crosshair. This means that this is an
adjustable part of the UI (user interface). Simply hold the
left-click and move your mouse up and to the left. The
viewport will expand on the fly. This is true for all bordering
lines in all four viewports. Experiment for a moment and start
scaling your different viewports. This is the fastest and most
flexible way to quickly adjust your viewports. If you are like
me, however, you don't always need to see all four views. You
may only want to work with two or three views. That means
we need to totally change our layout. At the upper-left corner
of all four viewports, as shown in Figure 2-8, you'll see the
name of that viewport (Top, Front, Left, Perspective).

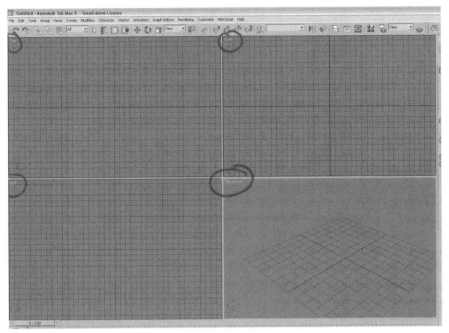

Figure 2-8: The viewport names are displayed in the upper-left corners.

If you mouse over the text and right-click, you will get a series of options.

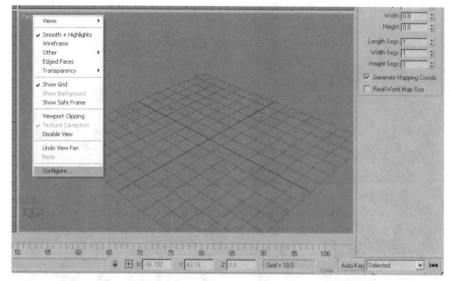

Figure 2-9: Right-click a viewport name to see a context menu with the viewport options.

If you go all the way to the bottom of those options and select Configure, a dialog box is displayed. The top of the dialog has a series of tabs. Select the Layout tab.

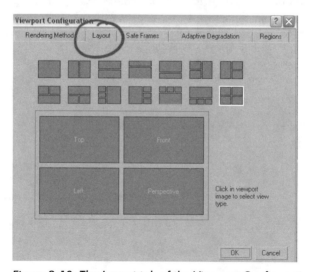

Figure 2-10: The Layout tab of the Viewport Configuration dialog.

This tab shows you a series of new layout options. If you select one of the different layout options at the top, Max will preview it for you in the window. Choose your desired layout and press the OK button. After pressing OK you'll notice that Max has updated to your new layout. Just like the default Max layout, this new layout can be adjusted manually.

Lastly, you can dictate which viewport goes where. That means if I want the Perspective viewport to be in the upper-left corner instead of at the bottom right, I can do that. Just right-click the name of the viewport you want to relocate. Instead of choosing Configure this time, select Views from the context menu. This will give you another menu that shows you all available views (Perspective, Top, Front, Left, Right, and so on). Just highlight the desired view and then left-click your mouse. Using these few viewport options gives you almost unlimited options for your user interface. As you progress as a 3D artist, you'll find that certain user interface layouts are more efficient depending on what you are trying to achieve.

Note:

Max automatically remembers your last layout. When you restart Max, it will return to the way you left it.

Customizing Your User Interface

Now we'll focus on customizing your user interface. Max is very user friendly, in that you can move portions of the UI around and even dock it to other parts of the UI. You can create your own custom toolbars and modify existing ones. We'll start off with the absolute basics. Let's start adjusting the current UI and moving things around a bit. The big command panel to the right of your screen is where you will access almost every tool in 3D Studio MAX.

Figure 2-11: The command panel.

This is what houses all your modifiers and their settings (among other things). The problem, however, is that sometimes a modifier or object has so many settings that you run out of room in this panel. When that happens, the excess settings are displayed below the other settings on the screen. Similar to navigating a long website, you have to keep scrolling down to see more information. This is not a problem, although it can become cumbersome to scroll down to the bottom of your settings over and over again. To accommodate the display of extended settings, you can pull this panel out horizontally. The settings will automatically adjust to the new room made available.

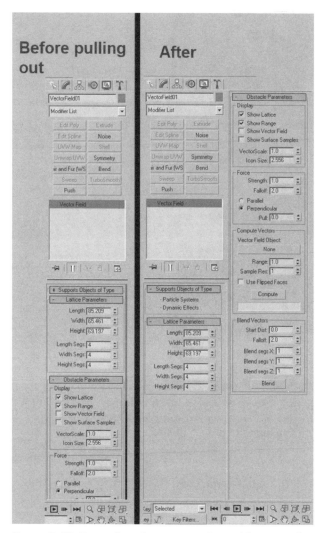

Figure 2-12: Expanding the command panel horizontally to display more settings.

To extend the panel just move your cursor to the left edge of that panel. Your cursor shape will change when you get to an adjustable area.

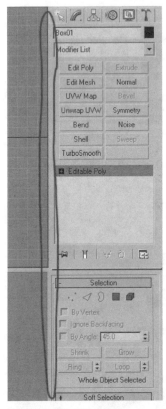

Figure 2-13: When your cursor is over the left edge of the panel, you can drag it left or right to expand or reduce its size.

Grab the edge and pull to the left. You can actually pull the panel out so far that you almost completely lose your interface.

You can also tear off parts of your interface and dock them to other parts of your UI or keep them as floaters. If you have dual monitors like I do, it's nice to tear off your command panel and put it on your second monitor. This way you can use one monitor as your 3D viewport and the other monitor to house all your tools. There are two ways to tear off parts of your UI. You can grab the corner of your panel and right-click. When you do that you will see a context menu with a few options (Dock and Float). You can also manually pull a panel off and move it about the UI.

Let's move a few things around for practice. Move your mouse cursor to the upper-left corner of the command panel. You'll notice that your cursor changes when you get to the correct place. When the cursor changes, you can right-click to float the command panel or you can hold the left-click and manually pull it off to the left. Pull the command panel off and keep it as a floater. Let's do this with the remaining toolbars by tearing off the top of our main toolbar next. If you move your cursor to the left of the main toolbar you'll notice your cursor change again.

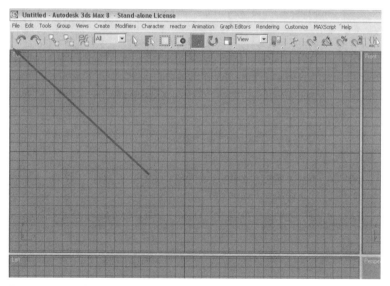

Figure 2-14: Move your cursor to the left side of the main toolbar.

Just as before, hold the left-click and pull the toolbar down. Now your main toolbar is floating as well. All that remains from the default user interface now is the set of Reactor tools to the left. What the heck, let's tear that off as well. Go to the top of that toolbar and tear it off just like you did the main toolbar. Your *entire* user interface is now floating.

Go ahead and start docking your toolbars to different sides of your interface. Simply grab the toolbar and manually move it to the left, right, top, or bottom. Move them around at random and practice a bit. Also notice that you can *stack* your toolbars. Take everything and dock it to the left of the interface. They will automatically dock to each other.

 Note:

You can take any horizontally docked toolbar and dock it on the side as a vertical toolbar and vice versa.

You can also create your own custom toolbars. Let's add a custom toolbar as a floater. Go to the top of the UI and, from the Customize menu rollout, select Customize User Interface.

Figure 2-15: Choose Customize User Interface to open a dialog box.

This will bring up the Customize User Interface dialog. We want to first create a new toolbar. Select the New button.

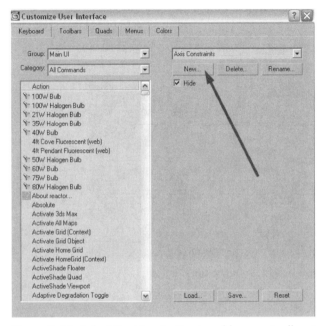

Figure 2-16: Select the New button to add a new toolbar to the user interface.

You will be prompted to name your new toolbar. Let's name it something totally random, like "Josh is a 3D Jedi." Max will float an empty toolbar in your interface.

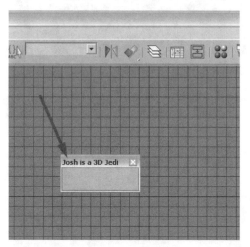

Figure 2-17: A new empty toolbar.

You can put absolutely any function in a toolbar. You can place a custom script into a toolbar or you can insert objects or modifiers that you use on a regular basis. As an example, let's put some modifiers into the new toolbar. If you go back to the Customize User Interface dialog you'll notice a long list of actions to the left. These actions are organized by categories. We want to add a couple of modifiers to our new toolbar. In the Category rollout, select Modifiers.

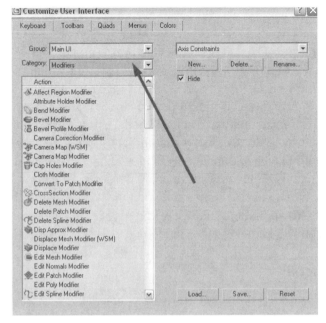

Figure 2-18: Choose Modifiers from the Category rollout.

You'll get a new list of actions in the Action list. Cursor over the Bevel Modifier action and drag it to the new toolbar. Next, grab the Cap Holes Modifier and drag it to the new toolbar. Go ahead and grab two or three more actions and move them to your new toolbar. Now that we have our new toolbar complete, we can dock it to any part of the user interface. This is now a functioning toolbar. The modifiers we added to it are working modifiers and act as buttons.

Once you get your interface layout the way you want it you can save it. To save your custom Max layout, go to the top of your Max UI and open the Customize menu. Left-click on Save Custom UI Scheme. Max will prompt you for a name for your new UI layout and a path to save the file.

Anytime you want to load a custom UI, go back to the Customize menu and select Load Custom UI Scheme. You will be prompted to select a custom UI to load. Select the UI of your choice and then select Open. This can be particularly helpful when you want to use different layouts for different tasks. If you are animating, you may want a layout that is set up for animation. Likewise, you may want a different layout if you will be doing more modeling.

 Note:

Max already has preset UI schemes: "ame-light," "ame-dark," modular toolbars UI, and Default UI.

Standard Primitives and Other Basic 3D Objects

Almost everything you create with 3ds Max will be based on a simple object. No matter how complex the render or how detailed the model, it's always a simple object at its core. 3D Studio MAX gives you a host of objects to start off with called standard primitives.

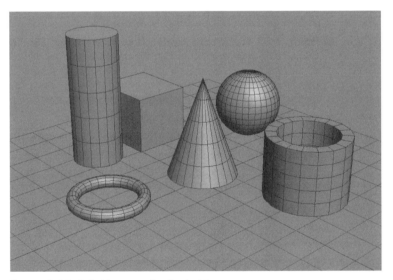

Figure 2-19: 3ds Max standard primitives.

These objects are located in the Create panel.

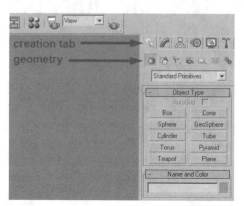

Figure 2-20: The Create, Modify, Hierarchy, Motion, Display, and Utilities tabs are located on the command panel.

Let's take a look at the standard primitives and how you will go about creating them in your 3D space.

We'll start off by creating a sphere. To access the standard primitives you want to make sure you're in the Create panel, as shown in Figure 2-21. Within that panel you want to make sure that the Geometry (sphere) tool is selected.

Figure 2-21: Choose the Geometry tool in the Create panel.

The geometry section of the Create panel contains several button options, including Box, Sphere, Cone, etc.

*Figure 2-22: The Standard
Primitives objects.*

3D Studio MAX works differently than other 3D packages in that you select what you want to create and then create it using a series of clicks on the screen. This is much easier in my opinion because you get to create the object where you want and the size you want right off the bat. Other packages will simply create your primitive at "zero" at its own generic size. You then have to move it to where you want it and also adjust its size. 3D Studio MAX avoids all this by letting you create primitives on the fly. With that in mind, let's create a sphere now.

Select Sphere in the geometry section. Now move your mouse cursor to your Perspective viewport (which should be the viewport on the bottom right of your screen). Next, left-click anywhere in the Perspective viewport and hold the left-click. You'll notice that if you continue holding the left-click and drag up and down you will manually change the size of your sphere. Create the sphere at your desired size and then release the left-click. Congratulations! You've just made your very first 3D object!

Note:

After you create your sphere you remain in Create mode, as indicated by your cursor. This means if you want to make more spheres you don't need to reselect the Sphere button; you just keep on making spheres now by using the left-click.

Make three or four more spheres at various locations and sizes in your Perspective viewport just for practice.

Now let's create a box. Return to your Create panel and select Box this time instead of Sphere.

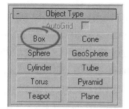

Figure 2-23: Choose the Box object button.

After selecting the Box button, return to your Perspective viewport and place the cursor at your desired starting point. Just as before, we are going to hold the left-click and drag the mouse. You'll notice that moving the mouse up and down has a different effect than moving left and right. A box requires more mouse clicks because it has length, width, and height information; a sphere simply has a diameter. After you hold the left-click, move the mouse around a bit until you get your desired box size. (Essentially you're creating the bottom of the box first. It should look like nothing more than a simple plane.) Release the left-click and move the mouse up and down. You'll notice that now you are affecting the height of the box. Move the mouse up or down to your desired height and left-click again to finish. That's it! Repeat this process several times. Try to make boxes of different lengths and widths.

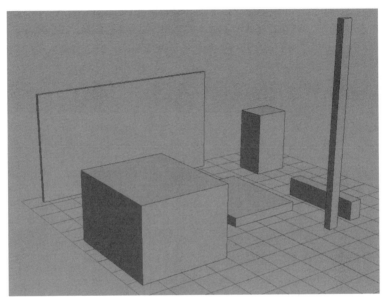

Figure 2-24: Boxes of several different sizes.

I'll let you experiment on your own with the other standard primitives. They are all created with the same principles in mind. There is even a teapot for you to create (long story behind that).

Extended Primitives

Extended primitives are just an extension of the standard primitives. Go back to your Create panel and access the Standard Primitives rollout. You'll get a drop-down with several options.

Figure 2-25: The Standard Primitives rollout contains additional primitives such as doors, windows, and extended primitives.

You can create doors, windows, extended primitives, and so on. Spend a little time in these three sections. The extended primitives are basic 3D objects just like the standard primitives, but they are designed with more of a specific purpose in mind. You can create a procedural hose on the fly and adjust its shape or how many rings it has. You can also create a "ring wave." This is something you might use if you were creating an explosion and you wanted a blast ring to emit from the center. Figure 2-26 shows a quick example of the extended primitives you have at your disposal.

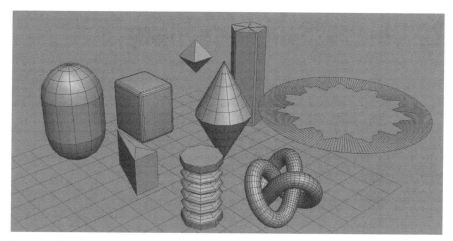

Figure 2-26: Examples of extended primitives.

Please take some time to explore the additional primitives. I would also encourage you to look under the Doors and Windows sections as well. Having the ability to create doors, windows, and stairs on the fly is absolutely invaluable and gives you more time to work on other things.

2D Objects (Splines and Text)

Even though you are working within a 3D software package, there are many times when you need to start by first creating a two-dimensional object. The two most common uses for 2D objects are when you are creating splines and when you are typing out simple text that you later want to extrude and give depth.

Figure 2-27: This two-dimensional text will be extruded later to give it depth.

In order to create anything we need to return to our almighty command panel on the right. Make sure you are in the Create tab of the command panel. Everything is created here, including your 2D splines. To access your 2D objects, select the Shapes tool in the Create panel.

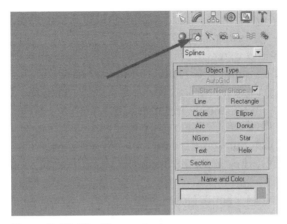

Figure 2-28: The Shapes tool.

In this new section you will see a list of 2D shapes you can create (circle, arc, star, etc.). Let's maximize our Perspective viewport as this is where we will create our 2D objects. Next, select Circle and return to the Perspective viewport. Hold the left-click and drag up to create your circle size. When you are finished, simply release the left-click. Booo-yah! A two-dimensional circle is born. (Very exciting, I know.) Most of your objects will be created with a single click and drag.

Next let's manually create our own spline instead of using a default shape. Go back to the Shapes section of the Create panel and select Line. Go back to your Perspective viewport and left-click once. That places your first vertex. When you move your cursor around now you'll notice a line is attached to it. Basically we are just connecting the dots at this point. Every time you left-click you will place a vertex. Just start clicking to create the shape that you want.

 Note:

When you initially create a spline it will have hard edges at all the corners. I will show you different spline options and how to use Bezier curves and handles to control your splines in Chapter 13, "Spline Modeling."

For now I just want you to be able to lay down a spline or other default Max shape.

Creating text works a little bit differently than the other shapes and splines. Go back to the 2D shapes in the Create panel and select Text this time. After selecting the Text object type, you need to type the text. This happens in the Create panel's Text area. (This is a great example of when you will want to pull out your Create panel in order to see all the options.) Either scroll down in the Create panel to see the Text area or mouse over the Create panel until the cursor changes into a hand. Now simply grab the Create panel and pull it up or down by holding the left-click. You should see the Text area with the words "MAX Text" inside it.

Figure 2-29: The Create panel's Text area.

This is where you will type your text. Delete the words "MAX Text" and type text of your choice. You'll notice that you have basic font options as well. After you have typed your text, left-click inside the Perspective viewport. Max will have created a spline version of your text. Now that you can actually see what you wrote in the Perspective viewport, you can go back to your text options and make any changes you want to the text. You can adjust the size, kerning, leading, font, and so on.

Time Slider

At the bottom of your Max UI you'll notice a series of numbers.

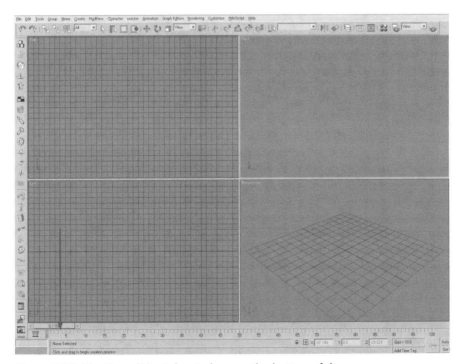

Figure 2-30: The time slider is located across the bottom of the screen.

This is your time slider, which is used for animation purposes only. Animators use the time slider to pace their animations and add or remove keys. This is extremely efficient for doing quick animation blocking or simple animations. It allows you to animate quickly without having to open the Curve Editor for detailed animation work.

Custom Colors

But wait! The fun does not stop there. You can also customize your UI colors in 3D Studio MAX. If you head back up to the Customize menu and select Customize User Interface, Max will bring up a dialog box. Select the Colors tab.

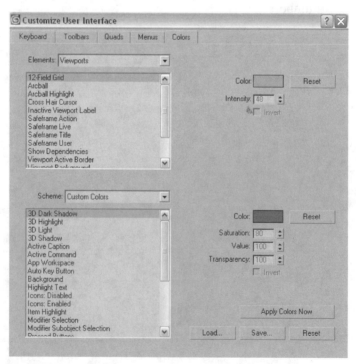

Figure 2-31: The Colors tab of the Customize User Interface dialog.

The Colors tab of the Customize User Interface dialog allows you to change just about every single color 3D Studio MAX applies to its UI and viewports. If, for example, we wanted to change the viewport background, choose Viewports from the Elements rollout. Then scroll down to Viewport Background. Highlight Viewport Background, then use the color swatch to the right to change the color. After you select the appropriate color, select the Apply Colors Now button.

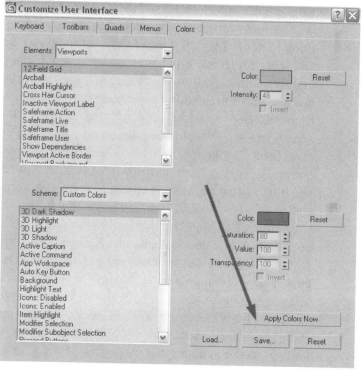

Figure 2-32: Click the Apply Colors Now button to apply your selected colors.

This will apply any color changes you have made. Just like all other customizations in Max, you can save these color settings using the Save button. After you have been using Max for a while you will no doubt want to change a few things to what suits your color preference best.

Creating Hotkeys

Creating hotkeys is not über important in the beginning. In fact, I often tell people to learn the program first and understand where everything is before they go butchering everything into their own custom setup. I am constantly frustrated at work when I ask very seasoned Maya users where a simple function is located and they cannot tell me. This is because out of the box Maya doesn't necessarily put everything in front of you. It doesn't gray out tools you don't need, and therefore doesn't highlight the ones you do need. You ultimately set up the UI to your liking and then it works very quickly. Max, on the other hand, gives you immediate access to most major tools via the default user interface. It only shows you what you do need, based on your given selection or sub-object. Because of this, the default UI is not only very fast but is also very consistent from artist to artist. You don't often run into a situation where you ask Max users where a tool is and they have to spend 10 minutes looking for it.

You will go about creating hotkeys in much the same way as custom colors and toolbars, etc. Return to the top of your UI to the Customize menu and select Customize User Interface. This will bring up our now familiar customization tabs. You want to make sure you have the Keyboard tab selected. Here you have a Group rollout, a Category rollout, and a list of things in that category. I am not going to have you change any hotkeys at the moment, but I would like for you to understand how it works so that you can do it when the time is right.

First you need to select the group in which you think your command is located.

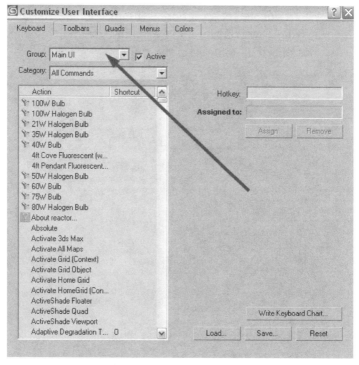

Figure 2-33: To create a hotkey, first select the group in which the command is located.

The Main UI group contains most of the navigation functions and viewport settings. If you wanted to create hotkeys for the Edit Poly functions, then you would need to go to the Edit-Poly group. For now, make sure you are in the Main UI group. Below the Group rollout is a Category rollout. If you know what category your function is in, you can select that category from the drop-down list. If not, then simply keep your Category rollout on All Commands. This will show you all possible commands in the Main UI group.

If you select an action in the Action list, you'll notice that it will show you any hotkey that it is currently assigned to in the Shortcut column on the right.

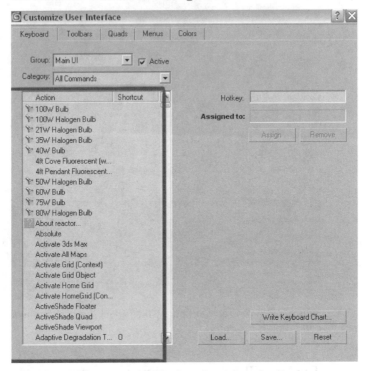

Figure 2-34: The Action list displays the current hotkeys.

Once you have found the action for which you want to create a hotkey, left-click on it to highlight it. To the right of the Action list are Hotkey and Assigned to boxes.

Figure 2-35: The Hotkey and Assigned to boxes.

After you select the action you want to hotkey, you simply left-click in the Hotkey box and press the key you want to assign. The Assigned to box will let you know if the key you have chosen is already assigned to another action. If it is, you can remove it by pressing the Remove button. Pressing the Assign button creates the hotkey. Bam! You are officially a customizing 3D ninja. Of course you have the option of saving your custom keyboard hotkeys. Just select Save (at the bottom of the dialog) and tell Max where to save it. You can also load any other keyboard hotkeys you have created in the past.

Modify Panel

The command panel is where you will access almost everything in 3D Studio MAX. It has several tabs that correspond to different areas of 3D. We explored the first tab (Create tab) earlier in this chapter. The second tab is the Modify tab.

Figure 2-36: The Modify tab opens the Modify panel.

The Modify panel is where all the little "goodies" are located. It's where you get to mess with the things you created with the Create panel. The default display of the Modify panel looks quite boring with not a whole lot going on. Max intentionally has kept all the modifiers listed in a rollout. This is not the most efficient way of working because there are quite a few modifiers. Sifting through them every time you want to get something is a bit of a pain. Max starts you off this way because it wants you to configure your modifier buttons yourself. You also have the option of choosing default configurations that aim toward a specific purpose, like modeling, animation, or mapping. These work extremely well and will take care of most of your needs.

To access the Modifier List rollout, you just click the drop-down arrow.

Figure 2-37: Click the drop-down arrow to see the modifiers.

You'll see a host of options. (If you don't have an object in the scene or any object selected, then you won't see any modifiers in the list.) These are all the modifiers available to you in 3D Studio MAX. As you can see, there are a lot of options and you may want to use a default button setup. To use a default button setup, put your cursor on the drop-down arrow and right-click. (Do not left-click the arrow.) This will give you a large list of options.

Figure 2-38: The list of default modifiers.

First and foremost you must make sure that the Show Buttons option is checked. Once it is checked, right-click the Modifier List drop-down again and select a button set. Let's go ahead and choose the Mesh Editing set. You'll notice that a large list of buttons shows up now under the Modifier List. These are the mesh editing options. This is a great setup when you are modeling. If the buttons are grayed out, it means that there is no object in the scene, so they are not usable. This is actually a very nice feature. If you are a Maya user, you know that Maya does not gray out unusable modifiers, which is very frustrating in the beginning because you don't know what buttons apply to what action.

Go ahead and sift through a few of the default modifier sets.

Adding Buttons to the Modifier List

After a while you may realize that you need to create a custom button set for your modifiers. To do this, just right-click the Modifier List again and select Configure Modifier Sets. This will pop up a brand-new dialog.

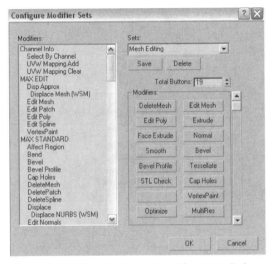

Figure 2-39: The Configure Modifier Sets dialog.

This dialog is very straightforward. You simply drag and drop what you want into your new list.

Just so that we are on the same page, make sure you have selected Mesh Editing from the Sets drop-down.

 Note:

In the future it does not matter what "set" you have selected. You can add or remove buttons no matter what is highlighted here.

Let's go ahead and get rid of a couple of buttons and replace them with something else. Go to your Modifiers buttons, and left-click and hold any desired button.

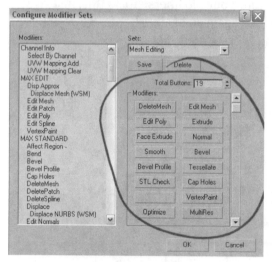

Figure 2-40: The Modifiers buttons.

Continue holding the left-click and drag the button back into the Modifiers list on the left. Max automatically removes the button, giving you a free space. Go ahead and get rid of a few more by dragging them into the Modifiers list. Also note that you can drag and drop anything anywhere. You can drag a button (up, down, left, right) to a different button position and so on. You can also drag an action from the Modifiers list on the left, and place it as a button to your right.

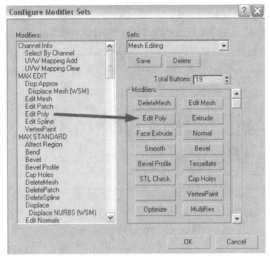

Figure 2-41: Drag an action from the Modifiers list
to make it a button.

After you move a few things around to your liking you may
still have a few empty slots left. Since there is no reason to
have empty slots, you can change your button count.

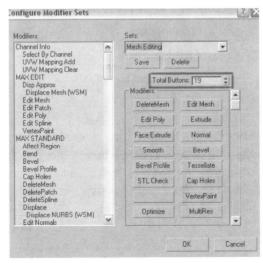

Figure 2-42: Change the number in the Total
Buttons box as needed.

Just raise or lower your button count to the desired number.

Being able to customize your button configuration is just another way to design your workflow around your personal needs.

Using the Axis Gizmo within the Perspective Viewport

The Axis gizmo is a glorious tool, my friends! This gizmo is what you will use to move, rotate, and scale everything in three dimensions. Unless you turn it off, the Axis gizmo is always displayed when using the move, rotate, or scale functions.

The Move, Rotate, and Scale tools are located together at the top of Max's user interface.

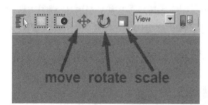

Figure 2-43: The Move, Rotate, and Scale tools.

Of course you must have something to move before you can use the Move tool, so let's create a box in the Perspective viewport. After creating the box, move up to the top of Max's UI and left-click the Move tool to activate it. If your box is not selected, just left-click it.

 Note:

The Move, Rotate, and Scale tools also act as selection tools, so left-clicking anything while using these tools will select the desired object.

Now that we have the Move tool activated and the box is selected, you'll notice that you have a gizmo with handles on it in the center of your box.

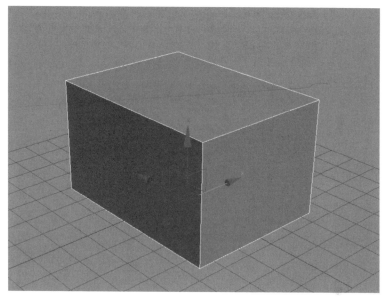

Figure 2-44: The Axis gizmo is displayed when you choose an object with the Move tool.

These handles show the X,Y,Z axes. If you want to move something on a specific axis, you would move your cursor over the desired axis (in this case it's X) and then hold the left-click. Start moving your mouse along the X axis. The box should be moving according to your mouse movements. If you want to move along a different axis, mouse over the desired axis. Hold the left-click and then move your mouse along *that* axis. Play around with the different axes. You can move things around very efficiently this way within your viewports.

✎ **Note:**

You can also move an object along multiple axes (or planes) at the same time. Your gizmo has two different sets of handles: single-axis handles and multiple-axis handles. To manipulate along multiple axes, simply grab the desired plane. In this image the X,Y plane is active and highlighted in yellow.

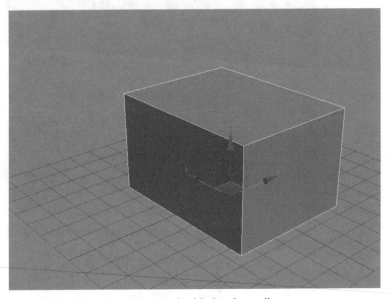

Figure 2-45: The active plane is highlighted in yellow.

Rotating an object works similarly to moving one. You have handles to rotate in a specific direction and you also have a free rotation, which allows you to rotate along multiple axes at the same time.

Make sure your box is selected. Move to the top of the UI again and select the Rotate tool (next to the Move tool). You'll notice your gizmo changes now to the Rotation gizmo. It should look something like this:

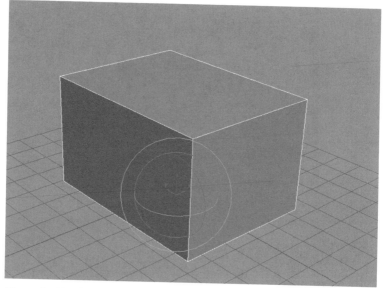

Figure 2-46: The Rotate gizmo.

The Rotate tool gives you five options for rotation: X, Y, Z, Free Rotation, and Screen Rotation.

You'll know which axis you are rotating around because it is displayed for you when you highlight the desired axis. Moving along the yellow line is the Y axis, the red line is the X axis, and the blue line is the Z axis. If you want to move around multiple axes, bring your cursor to the center of the Rotate gizmo. You know Free Rotation is activated when the center of the gizmo turns gray.

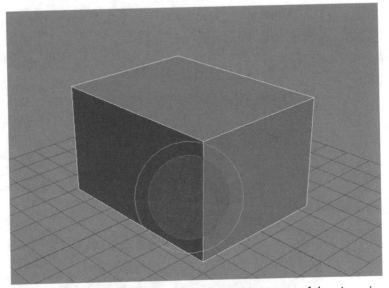

Figure 2-47: Free Rotation is activated when the center of the gizmo is gray.

Once Free Rotation is activated, hold the left-click and give your mouse a little spin. You'll notice the box react accordingly. With Free Rotation you can rotate around all three axes at the same time. This is a glorious tool.

You may notice that there is always a gray circle surrounding the entire Rotate gizmo.

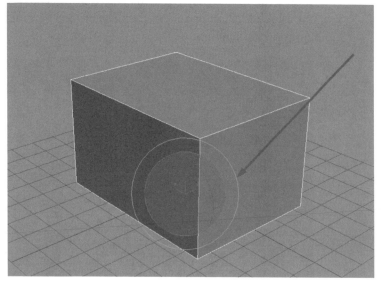

Figure 2-48: The Rotate gizmo can be extremely useful when you (the artist) want to rotate an object or objects based on your view of the scene.

This is your screen rotation. Screen rotation is just that: rotating your object parallel to the screen. This can be extremely useful when doing composites within 3D Studio MAX that are based on a stationary camera view.

Using the Scale tool should be very easy now that you know how to use the Move and Rotate tools. Select the Scale tool at the top of your UI. The Scale tool works exactly like the Move tool. You scale on the desired axis by grabbing the appropriate handle.

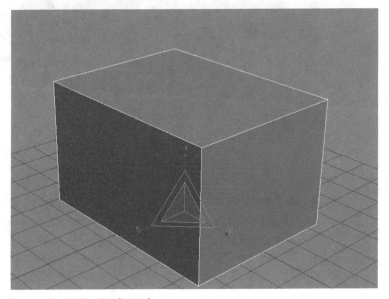

Figure 2-49: The Scale tool.

Similarly to the Move tool, you can scale along multiple axes by selecting an axis plane. You can also scale up in all directions by scaling in the middle of the gizmo.

Run outside now and go play with your new gizmo skills. Move, rotate, and scale to your heart's content. Then come back and we'll learn something else.

Adjusting the Size of Your Viewport Handles

You can quickly adjust the size of your gizmos by pressing the plus or minus keys at the top of your keyboard (not on the number keypad). Pressing the plus key will increase the size of your gizmo, and pressing the minus key will shrink it. Oftentimes animators want a large gizmo because they need to make changes quickly. This makes it easier for them to grab the gizmo and move or rotate around a desired axis.

Using the Modification Window to Edit an Object

We talked about the Modify panel earlier in this chapter. I want to go back to it for a moment to show you exactly how to apply a modifier and make changes to it.

Just so that we are all starting off on the same page, create a tube in the middle of your Perspective viewport. After you create your tube, go to the command panel to the right and enter these coordinates:

Radius: 10
Height: 75
Height Segments: 20
Cap segments: 1
Sides: 20

Perfect! Now that we have the world's most perfect cylinder we can add a modifier to it. Access the Modify panel and go to the Modifier List. Right-click the arrow in the box and select Configure Modifier Sets. A list of modifiers will appear. Under Object-Space Modifiers you'll find the Bend modifier. Left-click the Bend modifier.

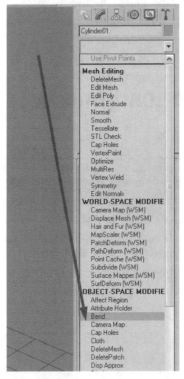

Figure 2-50: Choose the Bend modifier.

This will apply a bend to the top of your cylinder. Although we have added a Bend modifier to our cylinder, it looks like nothing has happened since the bend angle is set to zero. If you look in the Parameters section of the Modify panel, you'll notice you have bend settings (Angle, Direction, Bend Axis, etc.).

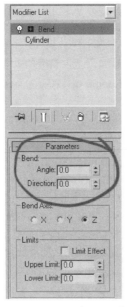

Figure 2-51: The Bend modifier's settings.

Adjust the Angle setting by placing your cursor on either the up or down arrow, holding the left-click, and dragging up or down slowly. You'll notice the cylinder is starting to wiggle a bit. Sweet, huh? Now drag upward until you are around an angle of 190. Your cylinder has a nice bend to it now.

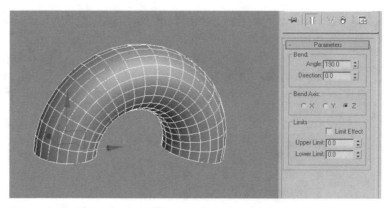

Figure 2-52: The cylinder with a Bend Angle of 190 degrees.

Go back to the Parameters area and adjust the direction of the bend. Hold the left-click over the up and down arrows of the Direction setting just like before and start sliding up or down with your mouse. I've been doing this a long time now and it still cracks me up to make a cylinder wiggle back and forth. OK, so I'm easily amused.

Time for the juicy stuff. Go back to the Modifier List and apply *another* Bend modifier to it. I know it's crazy, but just do it. Now your stack should look like this:

Figure 2-53: The cylinder now has two bends.

Just as before it, should look like nothing new has happened to the cylinder. So let's make some adjustments to our new modifier. Apply these settings:

Angle: –76
Direction: 0
Bend Axis: Y

You should have a wacky shape now that looks something like this:

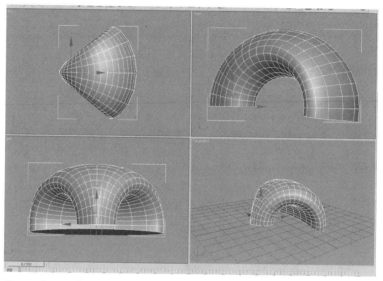

Figure 2-54: The cylinder with two bends.

Now the great thing is that everything is a modifier in your stack. This works just like layers.

If you have ever used Adobe Photoshop or any other program that makes use of layers, then you will understand how the layering works. In Max you can keep applying modifiers on top of modifiers. The modifier on top will affect everything underneath it in the modifier stack. This also means you can go back to the beginning and make changes. For example, let's select the cylinder in our stack.

Figure 2-55: Select the
cylinder.

This brings you to your original cylinder settings. Change
your original cylinder settings to have only six sides instead of
20. The bend modifiers are still affecting the cylinder, even
though we are at the beginning of the stack making changes.
Likewise, you can go to any modifier in your stack and make
adjustments at any point.

You also have viewing options available within your stack.
This is indicated by a small lightbulb next to your modifier.

Figure 2-56: The lightbulb
next to the modifier indicates
you can turn it on and off.

If you left-click this lightbulb you can turn that modifier on or off. This is a great way to toggle through your layers and decide if you like what a certain modifier is doing to your object. You can turn them on or off in any order you want.

You may also notice that next to your lightbulb you have a "+" sign. Clicking this will open your modifier and allow you to manually adjust that modifier via a gizmo. For example, select the Bend modifier that is on the top of your stack, then left-click the plus sign (+) next to it. This will open up your Bend modifier and allow you to actually select the gizmo in your viewports.

Figure 2-57: Left-click the plus sign (+) to open the modifier.

Left-click the word "Gizmo." Now if you go back to your Perspective viewport you'll notice that you can actually move the Bend gizmo around. Move it around and rotate it a bit. This is a nice way to add manual controls to an otherwise static modifier. Once you are done manually tweaking your Bend gizmo, you turn it off by reselecting "Gizmo" in your modifier stack.

Selecting Multiple Objects

There are a couple ways to select multiple objects in 3D Studio MAX: You can manually select them or you can use the Select Objects dialog.

To manually select multiple objects, just hold the Control key while left-clicking a series of objects. Create a few objects in your Perspective viewport and give it a go.

Once your scenes start getting more and more complex, manually selecting the things you want becomes nearly impossible. I've worked on scenes with upward of three million polygons, fifty-thousand objects, hundreds of lights, etc. Imagine trying to select the simplest of things in a scene like that. To get around this problem, you can use the object list in the Select Objects dialog. The Select by Name tool is located to the left of the Move tool at the top of your UI.

Figure 2-58: The Select by Name tool.

If you take a close look at the Select Objects dialog you'll see that it breaks down all the objects in your scene in the window at the left. The right side breaks down all possible Max objects into sections.

Figure 2-59: The Select Objects dialog.

Checking an object type displays those objects in the window to the left. By default, all boxes are checked, thus showing you *all* objects in your scene. If, for example, you had a large scene and you wanted to select all the lights in that scene, you would uncheck all boxes except the Lights box. The window to the left would then show you all the lights in your screen. You could then press the Select button at the bottom right of the Select Objects dialog. Bam! All your lights are selected.

There are a lot of ways to organize and efficiently wade through a very heavy scene using the Select Objects dialog. Let me just first say, *name the objects in your scene*. This is a good habit to get into for when you become a professional 3D artist and start working with other people. If you want to be a slob at home, that's fine, but when you start messing with other people's stuff, it's polite to be organized. (Stepping off soap box.)

If you know its name, you can just type the name of the object you're looking for in the top slot of the object list. You can also sort objects by type, color, size, and name to make things easier. To change how the object list sorts objects, simply change the Sort option in the upper-right corner of the window. At the very bottom of the Select Objects dialog there are a few other check boxes and buttons.

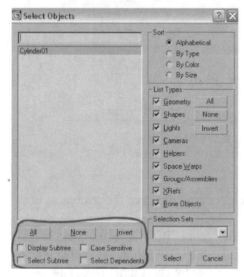

Figure 2-60: These buttons and check boxes allow you to further organize your object list.

You can quickly select All, None, and Invert selection using the buttons provided for you. Lastly, you can use the check boxes at the bottom of the object list to display subtrees, make the display case sensitive, automatically select subtrees, and select dependents. Some of these terms may seem a bit foreign to you at the moment, so don't freak out. You've got the basics and that's perfect for right now.

Understanding the Right-Click and How It Can Improve Workflow

OK, young 3D Jedis. One of the first steps to becoming a full 3D Jedi is efficient workflow. That way when your boss asks you to make a rock in 3D it doesn't take you two weeks. The three ways of creating efficient workflow are interface customization, hotkeys, and the right-click. Since we have already gone over interface customization and hotkeys, we need to explore the right-click a bit. Most programs have a "right-click" feature. They may call it something different, but they all serve the same function: to provide a fast way to access parts of the program without having to use a hotkey or going to the UI to get it. In 3D Studio MAX this function is in your right-click. To be honest with you, the right-click is entirely too broad for me to go over every single function and option. Instead, I am just going to point you in the right direction and let you explore it on your own a little.

The right-click in Max is hella-sweet! The right-click will show you different options depending on what you are doing and what you have selected in your scene. And, like everything else in Max, the right-click is totally customizable. You can find customization options for your right-click (aka quads) in the Customize User Interface dialog's Quads tab.

Make a sphere in your Perspective viewport and right-click it. You should see a context-sensitive menu that looks something like this:

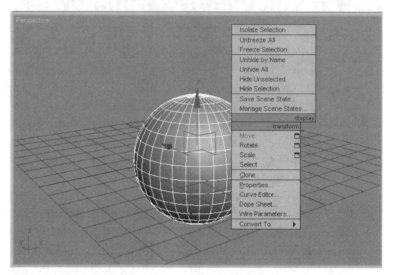

Figure 2-61: Right-click the sphere to see the context-sensitive menu.

Your right-click menu is broken up into two sections right now (it will increase to four sections, or "quads," in other cases). The top has display options such as hiding, unhiding, and freezing objects. The bottom has transform options such as Move, Rotate, Scale, and so on.

 Note:

Earlier in this chapter I showed you how to access the Move, Rotate, and Scale tools in the UI. Forget everything I said! Learn to access them through the right-click (or as hotkeys) to greatly improve your workflow.

For everything you are doing in Max, the right-click will update according to your actions. If you are editing a poly object, it will give you edit poly options. If you are editing a mesh object, it will give you edit mesh options. If you are sore, it will give you a back rub... OK, not quite, but it can do just about anything you want, and if it doesn't, then you can always customize it. In the next section we will start to get our feet wet with modeling. I will show you where your modeling tools lie in the UI and the corresponding tool in the right-click. After you know where everything is, I would suggest doing pretty much all modeling via the right-click. This is especially fast. You can even model in what Max calls "Expert mode."

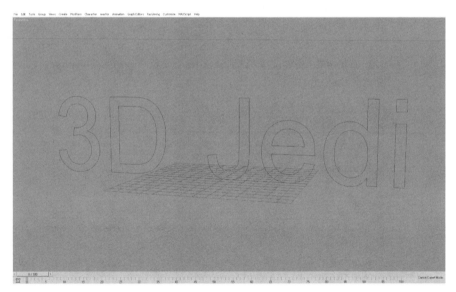

Figure 2-62: Modeling in Expert mode hides the UI.

When modeling in Expert mode, the UI disappears entirely and you do everything via the right-click. If nothing else, it makes you feel really cool!

Making a Copy or an Instance of an Object

The glorious work of copying! Imagine how bad life would be if you had to make 200 unique doorknobs. Not too fun at all, my friends! Thus the "copy" was born! If you want to copy an object in Max you simply hold the Shift key and left-click the object. You can also hold Shift and drag the object with the left-click. (Obviously, you need to use the Move tool for this.) Using the Move tool actually makes a little more sense because this way you can make a copy of the object and move it to where you want it all at the same time. Holding Shift and left-clicking will only create the new object directly on top of the original one. After doing a quick Shift + drag, you see a small dialog.

Figure 2-63: The Clone Options dialog appears after you Shift + drag to copy an object.

This dialog gives you a few basic but helpful options. You have the option of making the new object a copy, instance, or reference. (I'll explain the difference in a second.) You can also designate the number of copies you want made using the Number of Copies slider. Lastly, you can name the new object in the Name area provided for you.

Making an object an instance instead of a copy is extremely useful when you have similar objects in your scene. An *instance* is just the copy of an object on steroids; anything you do to the original object will happen to the copies. For example, when you are lighting a room it can be a good idea to create a light that you think looks accurate and then create an instance of it. That way if you turn the intensity of your original light down, the intensity of the instance will go down too. If you turn it up, the others will follow. This also works for editable objects. Any editing changes you make will happen to the instanced objects too. It is a glorious feature that saves you tons and tons of time.

A *reference* is the same thing as an instance, except that you can apply a modifier to a referenced object and it will not be applied to the original object, as it would with an instance.

Let's make a basic instance of a sphere as an example. Create a sphere and Shift + drag another sphere next to the original. When the Clone Options dialog appears, check the Instance option instead of the Copy option and press OK. The second sphere is now an instanced object. Select the original sphere, go to your Modify panel, and change the sphere settings. Adjust the radius and segment count. You'll notice that everything you do to the original sphere also happens to the instanced one that you made.

There are more advanced ways to use instances that we'll get into in later chapters.

Chapter 3

Modeling 101

How to Make a Standard Primitive an Editable Object

A standard primitive is simply an object with adjustable values. A sphere, for example, has an adjustable radius and adjustable segments.

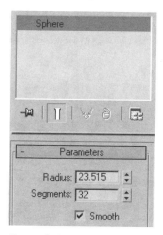

Figure 3-1

The sphere is not actually an editable object at this point. In order to make it an editable object, you need to collapse it to the desired editable object. There are many editable object types in Max, including Edit Poly, Edit Mesh, Edit Patch, and nurbs. All of them have advantages and disadvantages. Personally, I never ever use anything other than Edit Polys. If you have followed the industry for a while, then you have seen nurbs and patches come and go. Poly modeling has consistently been a fast and effective way to model most anything. Edit Poly and Edit Mesh are both polygon modeling; however, Edit Mesh is the old way of doing poly modeling. 3ds Max developed Edit Poly as a newer and faster way of modeling. It has all the same features of Edit Mesh, plus a lot more. There is no reason for anyone to ever use Edit Mesh these days. (It's an unwritten rule to never remove tools or features from a package; you only add tools and features. This is why Edit Mesh still exists in Max.)

To make a standard primitive an Edit Poly object, select the object and right-click it. At the bottom of your context menu you'll see the Convert To option. Highlight Convert To and a list of options will roll out. Select the Convert to Editable Poly option.

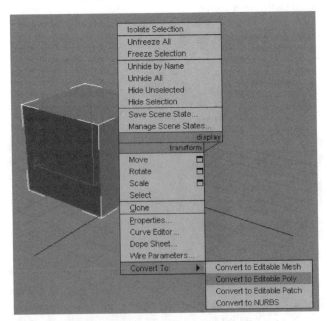

Figure 3-2: Choose Convert to Editable Poly from the Convert To rollout.

You'll notice that your standard primitive looks exactly the same; the only difference now is that you can edit the object with the available polygon tools.

Sub-objects

Sub-objects are what you actually use to edit an object. They are part of the object, just as my bones move me around but are separate objects inside my body. There are a few sub-objects that make up all poly objects: vertices/edges and polygons.

Let's all start on the same page. Create a cube in your Perspective viewport, then convert it to an Editable Poly object via the right-click menu. After converting it to an Editable Poly object, Max automatically takes you to the Modify panel. The Modify panel should look like Figure 3-3.

Figure 3-3: The Modify panel of the Editable Poly (cube) object.

A couple of notes about the Modify panel first. By default, all additional modifiers show up in the Modifier List drop-down. Max also allows you to work in "Button mode," which allows you to access buttons here instead of a drop-down. Button mode is much, much faster. You may be wondering, "Why would they set it up this way if it's faster to work in Button mode?" Well, Max does not presume to know how you want to work, so you have the option of loading button presets here (or customizing your own). To access Button mode, right-click on the Modifier List drop-down arrow.

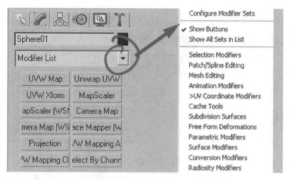

Figure 3-4: Choose Show Buttons from the Modifier List right-click menu.

Then choose Show Buttons from the list of options.

Now before you can edit any of the sub-objects or parts of your object, you need to select which sub-object you want to edit. Each one will bring up a different set of options and rollouts. Let's first learn to select different types of sub-objects. In the Selection section of the Modify panel, from left to right you have Vertices, Edges, Border, Polygon, and Element buttons.

Figure 3-5: The Vertices, Edges, Border, Polygon, and Element buttons.

Select the Vertices button. When you select the Vertices button, it should be highlighted in yellow.

Figure 3-6: The Vertices button is selected.

After doing this, you'll notice that your cube has small dots on its corners.

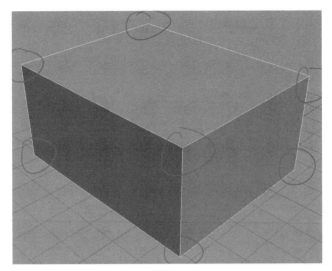

Figure 3-7: The dots on the corners of the cube are the actual vertices.

These are the actual vertices. In your Perspective viewport, select one of the vertices and move it around a bit. You can only *move* a vertex; you cannot rotate or scale it because it does not have a defined size or shape.

Next, go back to the Modify panel and select the Edges button.

Figure 3-8: The Edges button is selected.

You'll notice that your dots have disappeared. That is because we want to select our cube's edges now. Select at least one edge in the Perspective viewport and move it around a bit. Now try to rotate it and scale it a bit.

Note:

If you want to see the edges of any object in your viewport, press the F4 key. This will show a wireframe over your object, which can be very, very helpful.

Let's jump to polygons next.

Figure 3-9: The Polygon button is selected.

A polygon is just two triangles put together to make a square.

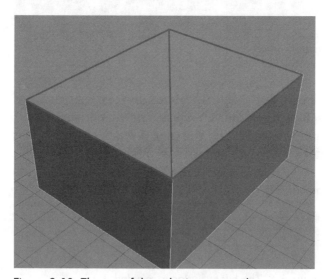

Figure 3-10: The top of the cube is now a polygon.

Each square is a "poly" or "polygon." Select the Polygon button in your Modify panel and then select one of the sides of your cube. The polygon should be highlighted in red. After selecting a polygon, practice moving it around. Also try rotating it and scaling it. After you are done moving your fun new polygon around, press the Delete key (assuming you still have the polygon selected; if you don't, then select the polygon and press Delete). Your polygon should disappear, leaving you with a hollow-looking object.

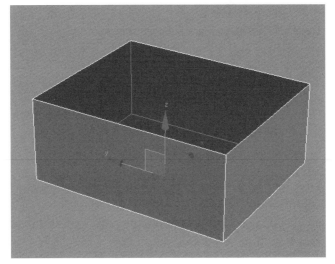

Figure 3-11: The top polygon of the cube has been deleted.

3D objects are not solid objects; they are simply shells and are always hollow inside.

Return to the Modify panel and select the Border button.

Figure 3-12: The Border button is selected.

Border is simply a very fast way to select an open set of edges. Select the Border tool and then select the hole we created earlier by deleting a polygon. Now you can move, rotate, and scale that hole to the desired size. This is just a quick way of selecting open edges. Before this option existed you actually had to select all the edges or vertices manually, which becomes *really* tedious over time.

Lastly, I want to show you the Element button.

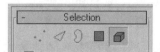

Figure 3-13: The Element button is selected.

The Element button is a fast way to select all polygons that are welded together. If you select the Element button and then select any part of the box in your viewport, the entire box highlights. This is a very fast way to select entire groups of polygons. When dealing with a small number of polygons or simple objects, it may be hard to see the benefit of such a tool. I assure you, however, as your object models become more complicated and busy, the Element tool becomes a life saver and saves you tons of time. Some packages still don't offer it as a selection option.

This is where it is important for you to just go nuts on your own and start "breaking stuff." Go crazy a bit and start playing with the different options in the Modify panel. Also explore those same options via your right-click menus. The right-click menus have the common functions associated with each sub-object built in for you. For example, if you select an edge and then you right-click, the bottom-left quad will give you a list of modification options available for edges. Selecting a vertex and right-clicking will give you vertex options, and so on. I urge you to get used to the right-click. If eventually you find some needed actions are missing, you can add them to your right-click menus.

Selection Tricks for Edit Poly Objects

I am going to show you some selection tricks associated with Edit Poly objects now. One of the best parts about using Edit Poly is the speed with which you can select multiple sub-objects. For example, create a sphere with a large number of segments (around 50). Collapse it to an Editable Poly object. Next, go to your Modify panel and select the Polygon button. Now go to your Perspective viewport and select a single polygon. After selecting your lone polygon, return to the Modify panel. You should notice under your sub-objects you have two buttons: Shrink and Grow.

Figure 3-14: The Shrink and Grow buttons.

These will grow or shrink your selection. Press the Grow button several times in a row. You'll notice that the number of selected polygons in your viewport grows with each click. Now press the Shrink button several times. Using the Grow and Shrink buttons is a very fast way to select desired areas of an object without having to manually go through and select specific sub-objects. For example, if I want to select a character's left arm, I would simply drag-select his left hand up to the wrist. Then I'd use the Grow button until the selection grew all the way up to his shoulder. This is much faster than manually selecting it. (The Grow and Shrink buttons also work when you are in Vertex mode or Edge mode; they are not just limited to polygons.)

Next, I want to show you how to quickly select edge rings and edge loops. It's difficult to explain what an edge ring or edge loop is without seeing it, so I'll just show you. Make sure you are in Edge mode and select a single vertical edge on the sphere. Now directly under the Grow and Shrink buttons you'll see two more buttons: Ring and Loop.

Figure 3-15: The Ring and Loop buttons.

Select the Ring button. Max will automatically select a ring of edges that go around the entire sphere.

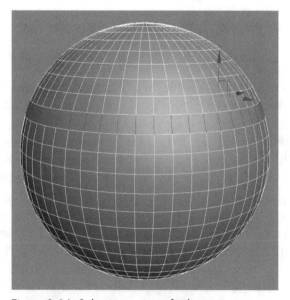

Figure 3-16: Selecting a ring of edges.

Basically the ring selection will keep going until it selects back into itself (like in our sphere example) or until it hits a *triangle*. Note the importance of triangles here. Triangles are something you should avoid unless you need to have them in your mesh for a specific reason. Try to model in quads as much as you can.

Deselect all edges now by clicking outside the sphere. Select any single edge again and this time press the Loop button instead of the Ring button. Loop will select a line of contiguous edges until it wraps back into itself or it hits a triangle.

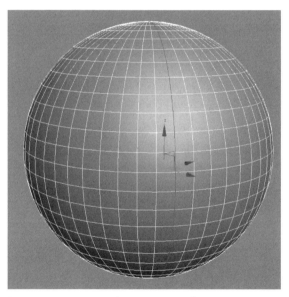

Figure 3-17: Loop selects a series of contiguous edges.

 Note:

TOP SECRET SELECTION trick that even very seasoned Max users don't know: You can quickly convert your selection from edges to faces or vertices to edges, etc., in Max using the Control key. Select an edge of the sphere and press the Ring button. Now, while holding the Control button, select the Polygon button in the Modify panel. This will convert your selection into polygons. Blam!!! (This one is worth the cost of the book all by itself.) You can keep pressing the Control button and go into Vertex mode now, or back to Edge mode, and so on. You can go back and forth between any sub-object mode you want.

Another cool new feature Max 8 has added is the ring and loop selection grow. You can now grow your ring selection and your loop selection just like you can grow a polygon selection. You do this with the up or down arrow next to the Ring and Loop buttons.

Figure 3-18: The Ring and Loop buttons now have increase and decrease arrows.

Soft Selection

On to one of my most favorite things on the planet: Soft Selection. Oh my gosh, what a glorious thing this is! Soft Selection is simply the ability to select a sub-object mode and have your movements affect the surrounding areas. Soft Selection also works in any sub-object mode (Vertex, Edge, or Polygon). Choose Polygon mode and select a single polygon on our trusty sphere that we are still abusing. Return to the Modify panel and locate the Soft Selection rollout.

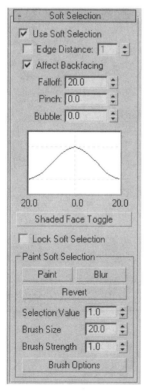

Figure 3-19: The Soft Selection area of the Modify panel.

(You may need to open the rollout if it's closed.) For right now we are keeping it über simple and really quick. I want you to click the Use Soft Selection check box at the top of the Soft Selection options. This will activate the Soft Selection mode. You'll notice that your sphere will show a gradient of colors around your selected polygon. Red represents a fully affected area, and it fades to green and finally blue after that. The closer to red it is, the more that area will be affected. Before we actually move anything, play around with the Falloff option a bit. Falloff is located under the Use Soft Selection check box.

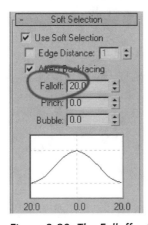

Figure 3-20: The Falloff setting.

If you scrub the Falloff up and down with your mouse, you'll notice the affected area update in real time in your Perspective viewport (cool, huh?). Just to make things a bit easier on the eyes, let's press the Shaded Face Toggle button.

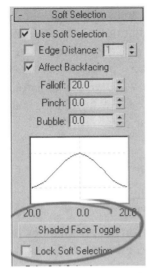

Figure 3-21: The Shaded Face Toggle button.

This does nothing other than make it a bit easier on the eyes to tell what areas are affected. Plus it kinda looks cool!

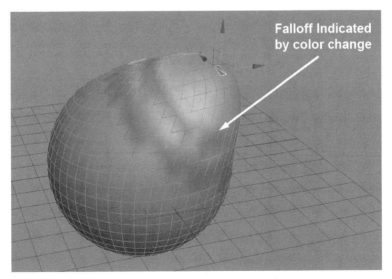

Figure 3-22: Shaded faces.

Go back to your Falloff setting and scrub it up and down again. You'll notice the shaded highlight updates in real time also. Finally, go into your Perspective viewport and move your selected polygon. You should be moving that selected polygon along with the surrounding area that you designated. Soft Selection is just cool. You don't know how lucky you are to have it because some major packages still don't.

Extrude Tool

Alright, now I want to blaze through several quick poly modeling tools that you will use a lot. First on the list is the Extrude feature. Delete our poor sphere and create a cube in its place. After creating the cube, collapse it into an Edit Poly object and go into Polygon mode. Then select the top polygon on the cube, and right-click your mouse. This will bring up a quad menu. The bottom-left quad houses the most common modification tools. Select the Extrude option.

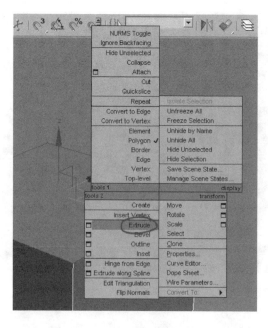

Figure 3-23: Select Extrude from the right-click quad menu.

It looks like nothing has happened; however, you'll notice that your cursor has changed. You are now in Extrude mode. Put your cursor over the selected polygon and, while holding the left-click, drag your mouse up and down. Sweet! You'll see that polygon going up and down with the movement of your mouse. Go ahead and raise it up and then release the left-click. Select any other polygon and repeat this process a couple of times. You can see how quickly we are able to extrude shapes off of our original cube.

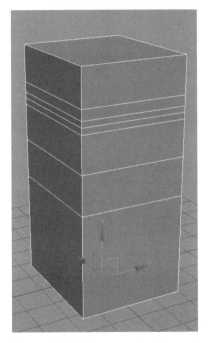

Figure 3-24: The top poly of the cube has been extruded.

I also want to take this opportunity to show you how to do this via a modification dialog as well. Select another polygon and right-click again. Go back to the Extrude option. You'll notice there is a small box just to the left of it.

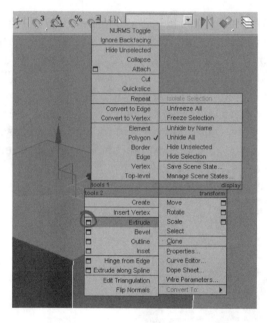

Figure 3-25: Click on the box to the left of the Extrude menu option to open the Extrude Polygons dialog.

Click that box and it opens the Extrude Polygons dialog.

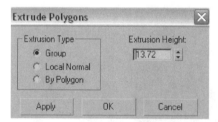

Figure 3-26: The Extrude Polygons dialog.

This dialog can be useful if you know a specific height that you want to extrude. This refers to the height of the extrusion itself, not the final height of the object.

 Note:

It also remembers your last extrusion height and will repeat that same height until you change it again.

Bevel Tool

Next is the Bevel tool. Bevel works a lot like the Extrude tool except it grows or shrinks the top of your extrusion. Grab any face on our cube (or create a new one if you need to). Right-click again. In the same quad as before, select the Bevel option.

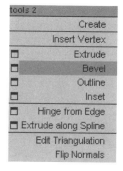

Figure 3-27: Choose the Bevel option from the quad menu.

Go to your highlighted face and, while holding the left-click, drag up and down again. So far it is working exactly like the Extrude modifier. After you get your desired extrusion height, release the left-click. Move the mouse up and down again. Now you're affecting the bevel. When you get the bevel to the desired size, you simply left-click again.

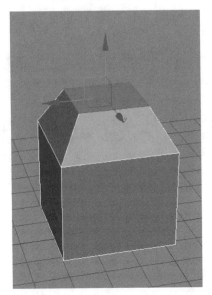

Figure 3-28: Using the Bevel option.

Try it again on a few more faces. Don't forget you don't always have to extrude or bevel up; you can extrude and bevel inward also.

Inset Tool

Next is our trusty Inset tool; yet another amazing tool that many packages don't have. It is basically a Bevel tool without the extrusion, as I'll show you next. Let's start with a fresh cube. Lord only knows what you have been doing to the previous one. Load up a new cube and choose Polygon mode. Select the top polygon and right-click. Select the Inset option in the bottom-left quad menu. Put your cursor over the selected face and, while holding the left-click, move your mouse cursor up. You should get something like this:

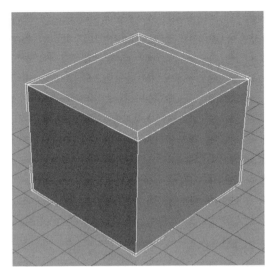

Figure 3-29: The top polygon has been inset.

Not the most impressive thing in the world, I guess, but what really makes the Inset tool shine is that it works around corners!

Start with another fresh cube and select the top and front polygons.

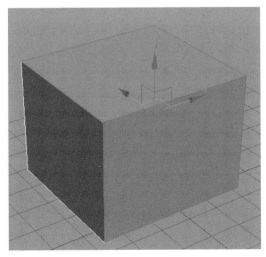

Figure 3-30: Select the top and front polygons.

Now use the Inset tool again. This time it repeats the same process but it actually works around the corner also.

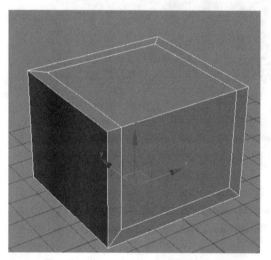

Figure 3-31: Inset corners with the Inset tool.

This is a *really* nice feature. Especially when doing mechanical or architectural modeling.

Hinge from Edge

Let's try the Hinge from Edge option next. Hinge from Edge does some cool stuff. It basically performs an extrusion while keeping a single edge welded to its base. Start with another shiny new cube. Grab the topmost polygon and select the Hinge from Edge option in your right-click menu.

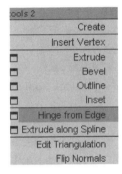

Figure 3-32: The Hinge from Edge option.

After selecting the Hinge from Edge option, your cursor will change. Put your cursor over any edge of the selected face. Your cursor will change to let you know you are in an active area. Hold the left-click and drag upward. You'll notice you're extruding that polygon but the edge you started on is staying welded to its base. After you have the desired angle, just release the left-click.

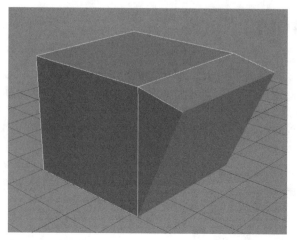

Figure 3-33: The polygon face extruded with Hinge from Edge.

Grab another edge and repeat this process. Do it a few times to different parts of the cube. You start getting pretty interesting results right away.

Connect Tool

Let's move on to my personal favorite: the Connect tool. This is pretty much the greatest tool ever created. (OK, I'm a bit dramatic, but I remember when you had to model without it.) Let's start with another new cube. This time add four segments to the length, width, and height so we have some things to play around with. Connect is simple; all it does is connect any selected edges or verts together. That's it. Choose Edge mode and grab an edge in the center of your cube.

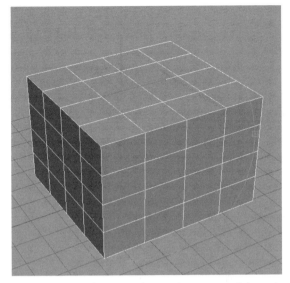

Figure 3-34: Select an edge in the center of the cube.

Now go back to the Modify panel and select the Ring button we used earlier in this chapter. Now your cube should look something like this:

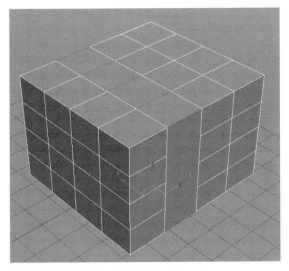

Figure 3-35: A ring of edges selected.

Right-click those edges and select the Connect option in your lower-left quad menu. Max will connect those edges together with a loop.

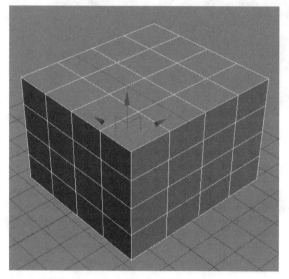

Figure 3-36: The ring of edges is now connected.

You can pretty much grab any series of edges and connect them to each other. They don't have to be in a straight line or anything in particular.

 Note:

You have to select edges near each other for the tool to work. If, for example, you selected one edge in the front of the box and one edge in the back of the box and told Max to connect them, nothing would happen. You'd have to select *all* the edges between the front edge and the back edge.

Now try the same thing with the vertices. Grab a series of
vertices and try to connect them. The figure below shows an
example of a series of verts that you can connect.

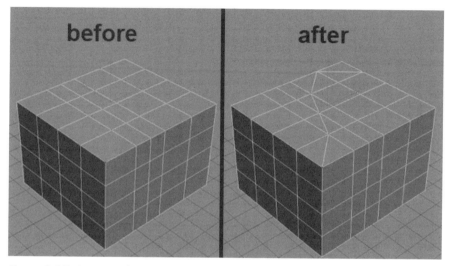

Figure 3-37: A series of vertices are selected and connected.

That little feature doesn't seem like a huge deal, but I gotta
tell you, it totally changes the way you model.

Insert Vertex

Next up is the Insert Vertex modifier. This one is really easy; you are just inserting a vertex onto an edge. Create a new cube and make sure you are in Edge mode. Right-click and select the Insert Vertex option in your lower-left quad. Next, bring your cursor over the desired edge and left-click to insert a vertex.

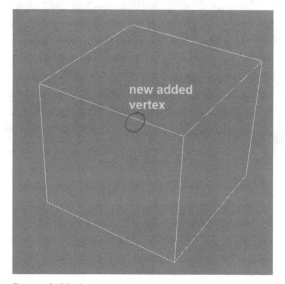

Figure 3-38: Inserting a vertex.

My only issue with this tool is that there is no visual feedback that you actually added a vertex. You won't see the new vertex that you made until you go into Vertex mode. This makes sense, of course, but I always thought there should be some visual feedback when you add a vertex. Until then, you'll just have to trust me that when you click Insert Vertex it does add a vertex.

Try to get creative now. Add some vertices and then connect them using the Connect tool. Then extrude a shape, etc. You'll start getting the feel for things soon.

Cut Tool

Max has several ways to cut and divide edges. One way is with the Cut tool. The Cut tool allows you to cut absolutely anywhere on an object. Thus, you can access it via any of the sub-objects.

Create another cube if necessary, and switch to Edge mode. (You don't need to actually select any sub-object of the cube; you simply need to be in any sub-object mode.) Once you are in Edge mode, right-click the cube and choose the Cut command from the upper-left quad of the context menu.

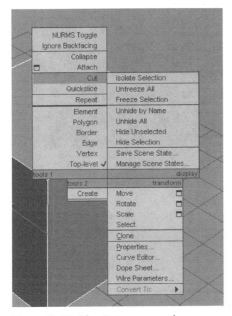

Figure 3-39: The Cut command.

Now move your cursor over your cube. Use the left-click to perform your cuts. You'll notice that your cursor will change, depending on what it is over (vert, polygon, or edge). Start left-clicking anywhere on the cube. Practice a bit going from verts, to polys, to edges. This is a very versatile tool and is something that you will use often. Go a bit nuts with it and just start creating cuts everywhere. You can see how quickly you can create your own shapes in a mesh using this tool.

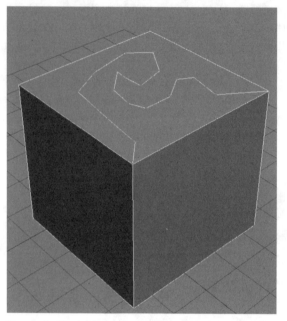

Figure 3-40: Adding cuts to the cube.

Chamfer Tool

The Chamfer tool is just another way to add more detail/cuts to your mesh. It is also a great tool for rounding out a hard edge. When you chamfer an edge, all you are really doing is doubling the edge count. If you chamfer a single edge, you are smoothing it out by dividing by two.

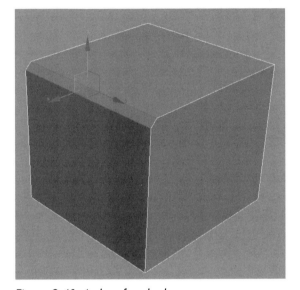

Figure 3-41: A chamfered edge.

Starting with a fresh cube in your Perspective viewport, let's use the Chamfer tool to smooth out one of the edges on the cube. First, make sure you are in Edge mode, then select the desired edge. In this case we'll select any of the top edges on our cube. After selecting the desired edge, right-click. You can access the Chamfer command in the lower-left quad of your context menu.

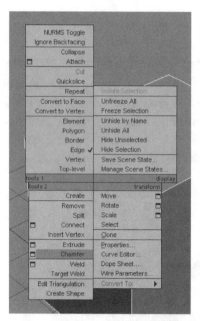

Figure 3-42: The Chamfer command.

Select Chamfer and place your cursor over the desired edge. While holding the left-click, drag upward. You'll notice you are splitting the edge in two and separating the edges while dragging upward. Once you get them to the desired distance, simply release the left-click. The cube should look something like this:

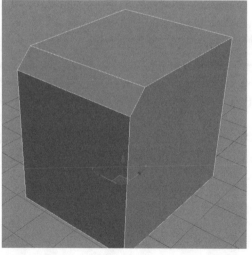

Figure 3-43: The edge has been chamfered.

Just like other poly tools, you can use this on multiple edges at the same time. For example, select the two edges you created. Right-click and choose Chamfer again. Place your cursor over either edge and drag upward while holding the left-click. This time you are chamfering both edges at the same time. Release the left-click when you get the desired chamfer. Your cube should look something like this now:

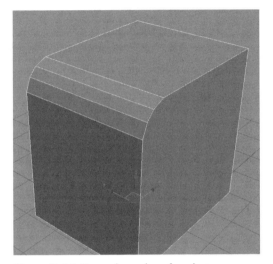

Figure 3-44: Two edges chamfered at once.

 Note:

The Chamfer tool is not limited to edges. You can also chamfer a vertex in 3D Studio MAX. Using the same techniques, try to chamfer a vertex on your own.

Bridge Tool

The Bridge tool has only one major function: to attach two open borders together by creating a bridge between them. This is a very powerful tool in 3D Studio MAX. After creating the bridge you have several adjustable settings for it, including Taper, Bias, Segments, and Twist. A great example of how to use the Bridge tool is when modeling a character's arm. It's not uncommon to model a character in pieces. You may model the torso and arms as a single piece, while working on the hand separately. After finishing the hand, you can position it and use the Bridge tool to connect the forearm to the hand. You can even use the Twist settings to get the proper forearm twist that naturally occurs when your palms face down.

We are going to use the Bridge tool at its most basic level. Create a single cube in your Perspective viewport. Hold Shift and drag a copy of that cube up in the Z axis. Your scene should look like this:

Figure 3-45

In order to use the Bridge tool you have to attach the two boxes as one object. But before we attach them, we need to make them both Edit Poly objects. Select both boxes and right-click. Convert them both to Edit Polys at the same time. Now select the top box and right-click. In the upper-left quad you'll see the Attach option.

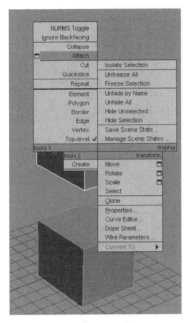

Figure 3-46: The Attach option.

Select Attach. You are now in Attach mode. When in Attach mode you click on any object(s) to attach them. You'll notice that your cursor changes when you go over the box on the bottom. Left-click to attach it. To get out of Attach mode (or any mode for that matter), just right-click. In most cases, this will bring you back to the Move tool.

Now that both cubes are attached together as one object, we need to delete two polygons in order to create the bridge. Delete the bottom polygon of the top cube, then delete the top polygon of the bottom cube, as shown in Figure 3-47.

Now we can actually create our bridge. Select the Border sub-object in your Modify panel, then select the open borders on both cubes, as shown in Figure 3-48.

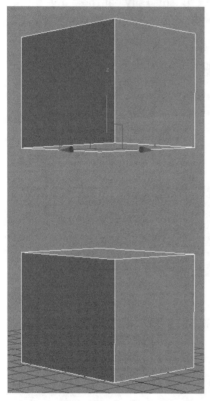

Figure 3-47: Delete the bottom poly of the top cube and the top poly of the bottom cube.

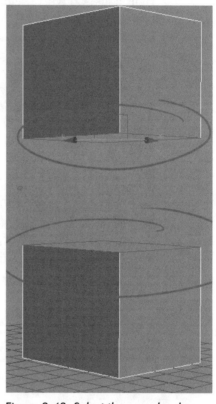

Figure 3-48: Select the open borders.

Return to your Modify panel and select the Bridge button.

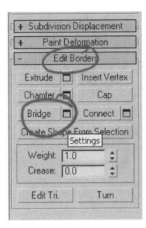

Figure 3-49: Select the Bridge button from the Modify panel.

You can simply use the Bridge tool to connect two borders, but as with most modifiers, if you want to adjust your bridge, you need to open its dialog to access extra settings.

After pressing the Bridge button, your cubes should be connected now with a bridge. Try this again, only this time instead of pressing the Bridge button, press the button for the Bridge Borders dialog next to it (the button with the square on it). You'll get several settings for your Bridge tool. You can add or remove segments, and adjust your taper, bias, and smoothing. On the left side of the dialog you have twist options.

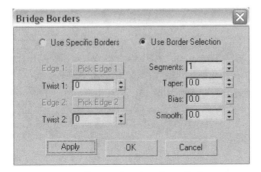

Figure 3-50: The Bridge Borders dialog.

Place a 1 in the Twist 1 setting area and click Apply. This will twist your bridge one time from one end of the bridge to the other. Now if you were to add segments to your bridge and also adjust your taper, you would have a totally different looking bridge, perhaps something similar to the following:

Figure 3-51: Add segments and adjust the taper of the bridge.

Play around with the tool until you get used to all the settings. As I said in the beginning, the Bridge tool is powerful. If nothing else, it saves you from having to do such tedious things yourself.

Attaching Objects

We actually covered how to attach objects in the previous section, but I wanted to go over it one more time. First of all, what does attaching two objects do? Well, if I have two spheres and I attach sphere A to sphere B, then Max will now consider them a single object. Attaching is not "linking" two objects; that is something totally different.

There are two ways to attach objects together in Max: You can do it manually by clicking the objects you want to attach, or you can use your object list to do it. You would only want to use your object list in cases where you have many things to attach.

Let's quickly create several objects in order to attach them together. Create a sphere in your Perspective viewport. After creating your sphere, hold the Shift key and move the sphere to your left. Release the left mouse button. This pops up your Copy dialog box. Normally you would just press OK, but we actually want multiple copies of this sphere. Up the Number of Copies setting from 1 to 12 and press OK. This copies the sphere to the left 12 times. Select any one of the spheres and right-click. In the upper-left quad, select the Attach option. You are now in Attach mode. Any object you left-click on thereafter will be attached to the selected object. Also notice that your cursor changes when you place it over an attachable object. I want you to attach any five spheres.

Right-click to leave Attach mode. (Right-clicking will take you out of just about any mode in Max. In most cases it brings you back to the Move tool.) You should now have six remaining spheres that need to be attached to the others. Let's use the object list for the last six. Right-click any sphere in the scene again. In your upper-left quad you'll notice a small box next to the Attach option.

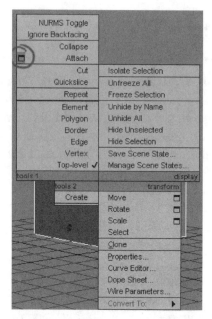

Figure 3-52: Click on the small box next to the Attach option to open the object list.

Select the small box to bring up your object list. The object list simply lists every object that is in your scene. Highlight everything in your object list and press Attach at the bottom right of the window. Max automatically attaches all selected objects and then closes the window. All the spheres in your scene should now be a single object.

Chapter 4

Creating a Basic Material

Before I get too far into modeling I want to start talking about materials in 3D Studio MAX. There are a lot of pretty funny misconceptions about how materials are made in 3D applications. If you're like me, it's usually some crazy family member at Thanksgiving asking questions about what you do for a living. "So you just draw on paper and then, like, 'scan' it into the computer or something, right?" I've even been asked if we draw straight on our monitor. The most popular one is "scan." People are not sure what or how you "scan" something into the computer, but they are sure it happens a lot. Maybe they think it's like the movie *Weird Science*, where we just feed photos and magazines into a "scanner" and the computer builds stuff for us.

The realities are much different, however. Creating a texture in any 3D application works very similar to the way a painter works, in that you have layers. Just like a painter has to start with a color layer and then build up from it, we have to start with a base layer and then add what we want to the material properties. For example, if we want something to be shiny, we can't just expect it to be shiny. We have to very specifically dictate how shiny it is, where the shininess is applied, and so forth. We do this by creating a grayscale map that will dictate the shininess. There are a million little tricks and techniques that can be used to create your materials. Some we will explore in this book; others that are a little more obscure you will have to research or discover on your own.

Accessing the Material Editor

To access the Material Editor, click on the Material Editor button in the upper-right side of your UI.

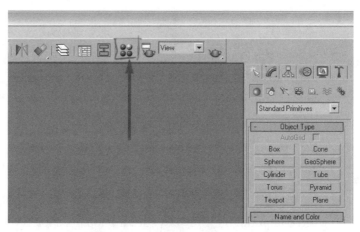

Figure 4-1: The Material Editor button.

Pressing this button will open the Material Editor.

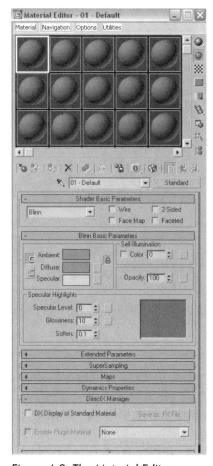

Figure 4-2: The Material Editor.

The Material Editor is broken up into a few major sections. At the top of the Material Editor you will notice several spheres.

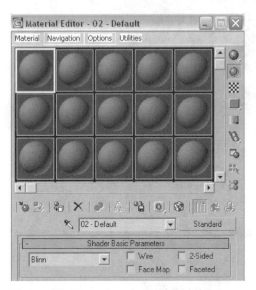

Figure 4-3: The spheres at the top of the Material Editor display the existing shaders.

These are empty shaders that you will eventually use to preview your custom shader or material before you apply it to the objects in your scene. Everything below that part of the Material Editor is a specific parameter rollout that you can use to create your own custom material.

Note:

Double-clicking on a shader will bring up a larger viewing window.

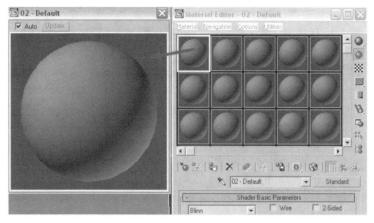

Figure 4-4: Double-click on one of the spheres to see it in a larger window.

This new window is adjustable. Just grab either bottom corner and drag it up or down in size. The larger you drag this window, however, the longer it will take to refresh your material updates. Likewise, you can right-click a shader and adjust your viewing size.

Applying an Empty Material to an Object

Before I get into the nuts and bolts of the Material Editor, you need to know how to do the most basic thing: apply a texture to an object in your scene. There are a couple ways to apply a texture to an object. You can use the Apply Material to Object button, or you can simply drag the material from the editor and drop it onto the object. Max is very user friendly and allows for a lot of dragging and dropping, especially within the Material Editor. I'll show you how to apply a material using both techniques.

First, create two objects in the Perspective viewport that you can use for applying textures. Select either one of the objects in your Perspective viewport, then select any material in your Material Editor.

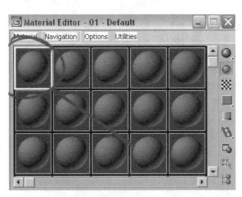

Figure 4-5: Select one of the shader materials.

You know that you have a material selected because it will have a white border around that material slot. After selecting your material, click the Apply Material to Object button.

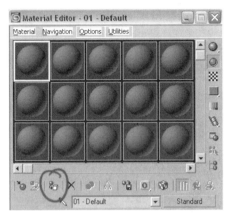

Figure 4-6: Click on the Apply Material to Object button.

This applies the selected material to the selected object in the scene.

Next let's try the drag and drop method. Select a different material in your Material Editor. Now, while holding the left-click, drag that material directly on top of the second object in your Perspective viewport. Releasing the left-click applies the material.

Note:

Sometimes you create so many materials and make so many changes that you forget if you're using certain materials or not. Fortunately, Max lets you know that a material is being used in your scene by graying out the four corners of your shader.

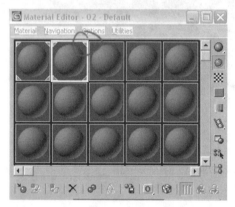

Figure 4-7: The gray corners of the material indicate it is used in the scene.

Changing Colors

If we pick up right where we left off, you should have a scene with two objects in the Perspective viewport that have materials already applied to them. All we want to do now is change the color of the shader via a color swatch. The color swatch is located at the top of the Blinn Basic Parameters rollout.

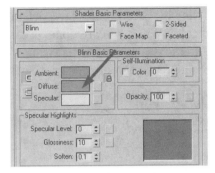

Figure 4-8: The color swatch.

Selecting this color swatch (also referred to as the diffuse channel) brings up a color adjustment window that is pretty standard in most any multimedia package.

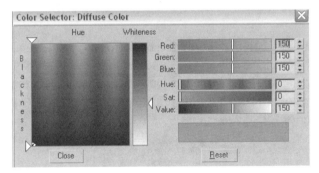

Figure 4-9: The Color Selector window for diffuse color.

If you know the exact color value you want, you can type it in the boxes to the right. Otherwise, you can use the large color swatch to the left to manually select the color. Place your cursor inside the colored area and click or drag the cursor until you get the desired color.

Select either of the objects and adjust the default gray color to a bright red color. When you are done, press OK. Pretty simple stuff. You may also notice that when you change the diffuse color, the ambient color changes with it.

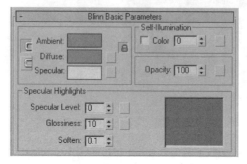

Figure 4-10: When you change the diffuse color of a material, the ambient color changes as well.

Ambient color is simply the background or surrounding color. By default, 3D Studio MAX locks these two colors so they are the same. If, for some reason, you ever want a different ambient color from your diffuse color, just press the Lock button to unlock these two colors.

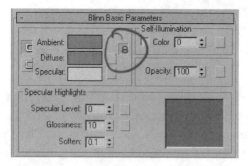

Figure 4-11: Lock and unlock ambient and diffuse colors with the Lock button.

Now you are free to adjust the ambient and diffuse colors independently of each other.

Adjusting Specular Levels and Glossiness

Different materials have different levels of shininess. If you are making a cloth texture, for example, you want a very low level of shininess because cloth absorbs light. If you were making a polished marble texture, then of course you would want it to be very glossy. To make simple adjustments to your material's specular highlights and glossiness, open the Material Editor. In the Blinn Basic Parameters rollout you have a few basic options. Let's focus on the Specular Highlights area.

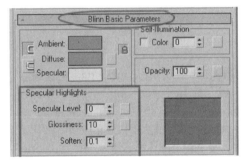

Figure 4-12: Adjust the Specular Highlights settings of a material in the Blinn Basic Parameters rollout.

Everything in the Material Editor works on a spinner. You can type the desired number or you can drag the spinner up or down using the left-click. To add a higher specular level to your material, increase the Specular Level setting.

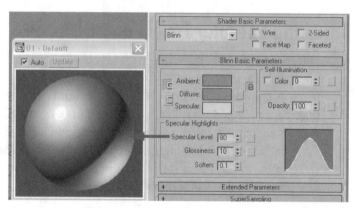

Figure 4-13: A material looks shinier with a higher specular level.

By default it will start at 0, which means it has no highlight. Increase the Specular Level setting to 80 or 90. You'll notice that the ball becomes a bit blown out. That is because we increased the specular level very significantly. To fix this blown-out look, we will need to adjust the glossiness. Just under the Specular Level setting, you have the Glossiness spinner. Increase your Glossiness setting to 30. You'll notice this brings the highlight to a point.

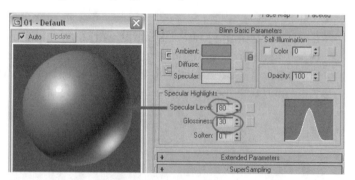

Figure 4-14: Increase the Glossiness setting when you increase the Specular Level setting.

Now the material looks much like a marble ball. You also have a Soften setting underneath the Glossiness setting. Increasing the Soften amount will do just that — it will soften your highlight.

Self-Illumination and Opacity

Sometimes you want a material to generate its own illumination. This will brighten the material and also give it more of a flat look. Imagine you have a solid sphere with a light source inside of it. This is what the Self-Illumination setting does.

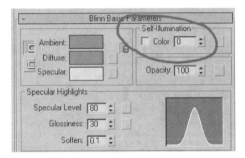

Figure 4-15: The Self-Illumination setting.

By increasing the Self-Illumination setting you should notice the material get brighter.

Opacity is a fancy word that refers to an object's transparency. You can adjust an object's opacity by using the Opacity setting.

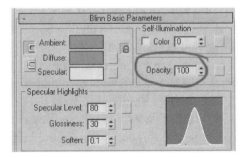

Figure 4-16: The Opacity setting.

Drag the spinner up and down to make the object become more and less transparent.

✎ **Note:**

Because there is no background in your Material Editor, it may look like nothing has happened. To add a default Max background, select the small checkerboard image at the upper-right side of your Material Editor.

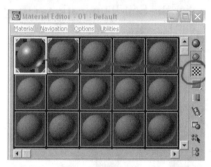

Figure 4-17: Adding a default background.

This will add a checkered background to your selected material.

Adjusting the Shader Type

Most 3D applications have default shader types. Certain shader types work better for certain results. Some allow for multiple highlights, and others absorb light better for skin textures. Basically, they are preset material types that give you a good starting point when creating your own materials.

I don't want to get into a lot of detail regarding shader types right now, but rather show you where they lie in the editor and let you explore a bit on your own. In the beginning it's not very critical to use anything other than the default shader type (called Blinn). As your skills progress within the Material Editor, you will inevitably explore these on your own.

The different shader types are located in the Shader Basic
Parameters rollout.

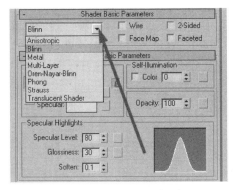

*Figure 4-18: Choose preset shader types
from the Shader Basic Parameters rollout.*

If you open the shader types list, you'll find a number of different shader options. Some of these are fairly obvious (Metal
and Translucent Shader), while others are a bit more obscure
sounding. Play around with each shader type on your own. In
most cases, the basic parameters won't even change; the only
thing that actually changes is the way your new shader reacts
to outside influences such as light.

Using the Maps Rollout to Add Realism

Now that we've got the basics out of the way, we can get to the really nitty-gritty stuff. First of all, let's open the Maps rollout so I can explain what you are looking at.

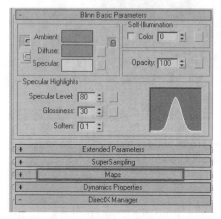

Figure 4-19: Click on Maps to open the Maps rollout.

This will open up a long list of empty slots along with their corresponding names and spinners.

Figure 4-20: The default Maps rollout.

The names to the left let you know what channel you are
working in. The spinners and empty map slots to the right are
what you will use to modify that channel. Map channels often
rely on images. You can use a color image or a black and white
image. For your diffuse layer (color channel), you would obviously want to use a color texture, but for most others, you
would want to use a black and white image. 3D packages use
black and white images to assign properties; white is positive
and black is negative. A very basic example of this would be if
I created a black and white checkerboard pattern and placed it
into the Bump channel of my Maps rollout. The bump I would
get as a result of this would be everything that is white would
be "raised" and everything that was black would be
"lowered."

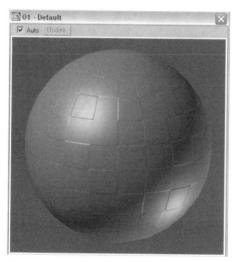

*Figure 4-21: Adding a black and white
Bump channel.*

This rule applies to almost all channels. Just remember, white
is positive and black is negative. Once you start to understand
the map channels and how they affect each other, you can very
quickly come up with very real-looking textures.

Loading Textures into Specific Map Channels

To load a texture into a desired map channel, just click on the appropriate empty slot. In this example let's load an image into the Diffuse Color slot.

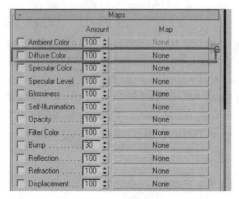

Figure 4-22: Choose the Diffuse Color map channel.

This will bring up a very long and scary-looking window of presets.

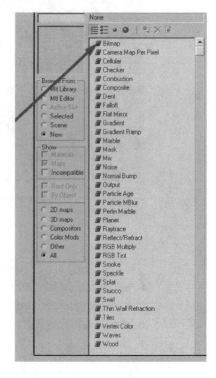

Figure 4-23: Clicking on the empty Diffuse Color map channel opens a window containing presets.

These are all presets that you can use, and I urge you to play around with them. For now, however, we want to select the Bitmap option.

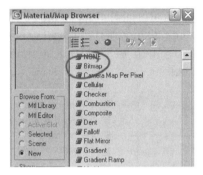

Figure 4-24: Choose the Bitmap preset.

This means I simply want to use an image in my map channel. Selecting Bitmap will open a normal Windows browser. Find the desired bitmap and select OK.

This is the part where I really want you to just go in and break stuff. I will give you a quick example of how to create a bump using the Bump channel. After that, I want you to explore the Material Editor on your own. Load things into various slots and just watch the results. You will learn a lot that way.

How to Create a Bump Effect Using the Bump Channel

Let's create a very basic material that has a nice bump map in the Bump channel. Create a shiny red material using the Blinn Basic Parameters rollout. Then let's add our bump map. Select the empty Bump channel.

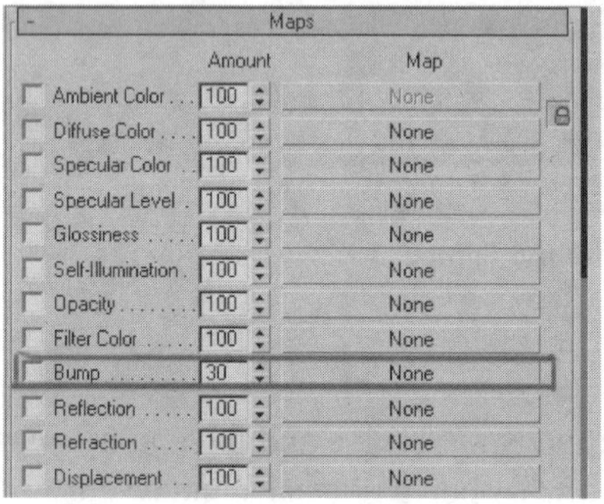

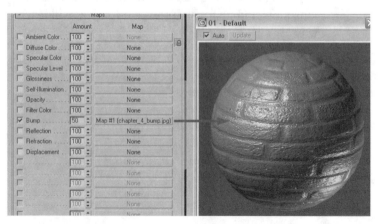

Figure 4-25: Select the empty Bump map channel.

Select the chapter_4_bump.jpg image from the book's companion files (available at www.wordware.com/files/3dsmax). You'll notice that the bump immediately takes effect on the sphere in your material slot. Cool, huh?

Figure 4-26: As soon as you assign an image to the Bump channel, it is displayed on the material.

You'll also notice that anytime you enter a bitmap into an empty slot, it takes you into a totally new section of the Material Editor.

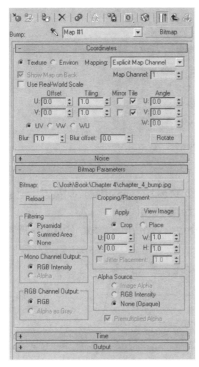

Figure 4-27: The Coordinates and Bitmap Parameters rollouts open when you add an image to an empty map.

All channels have their own little individual editors. They are very easy to navigate and can really help you get those final little tweaks you want. Notice you have a Coordinates rollout.

Figure 4-28: The Coordinates rollout.

Here you can adjust the texture's offset, tiling, and so on. You can even blur the texture right here in Max.

Below the Coordinates rollout is the Bitmap Parameters rollout.

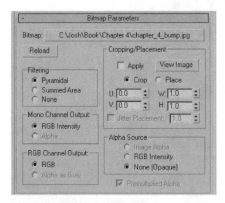

Figure 4-29: The Bitmap Parameters rollout.

This simply tells you where the texture is located. You can preview textures here using the View Image button.

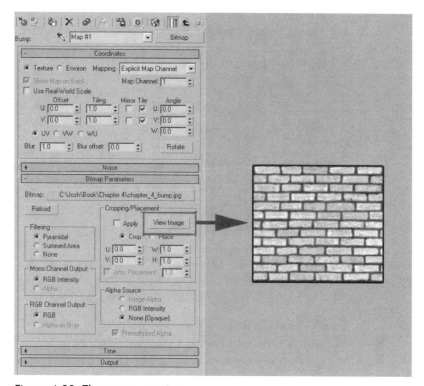

Figure 4-30: The texture preview.

You can also crop images very quickly using the Cropping/Placement group of settings. Check the Apply option, then select the View Image button. Within your viewer, adjust the viewable area. The Place option lets you place the image at an exact location.

If this image had an alpha channel, we could tell Max to use that alpha channel by selecting the Image Alpha option in the Alpha Source group.

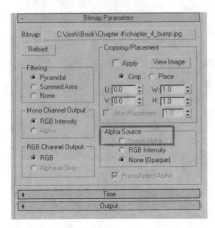

Figure 4-31: If the image contains an alpha channel, tell Max to use it by choosing Image Alpha.

These are just a few really fast ways to make quick texture adjustments without having to flip back and forth to Photoshop or a similar package to do things like tile adjustment and cropping.

To close this section of the Material Editor, click the Go To Parent button located in the upper-right corner.

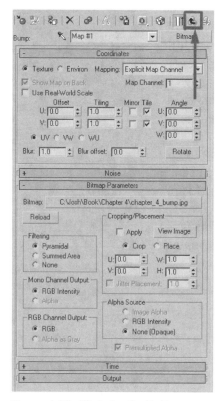

Figure 4-32: Click the Go To Parent button.

Repeatedly pressing that button will take you back to the original Material Editor layout, as shown in Figure 4-2.

Note that the spinner next to the Bump channel is set to 30, as shown in Figure 4-33.

This is where you adjust your intensity settings. Up the number to 60. Next try 120. You'll see the bump starting to get a little out of control at that level. This is a great example of how to use your map channels and spinners at their most basic levels.

If you ever want to go back into the Bump channel and make adjustments or use a new map, click on the bump slot again. This will take you back to the options portion of the Bump channel.

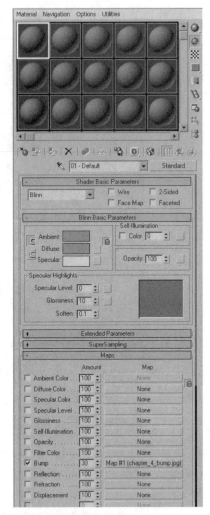

Figure 4-33: Adjust the Bump channel setting.

Chapter 5

Adding Lights to Your Scene

Understanding the Importance of Lights in a 3D Environment

Light plays a very important part in creating a convincing 3D model or scene. Without light, your 3D objects can appear as flat as a sheet of paper. If a sphere didn't have a "hot spot" of light, you wouldn't know it was round. If a box didn't have a shadow beneath it, you wouldn't know that it was sitting on the ground. Light attaches objects to the scene and is essential when creating a 3D scene.

Many new artists focus so hard on creating materials or models that they fail to pay enough attention to lighting. What they don't realize is that in order for you to properly showcase your 3D models, you must have good lighting. I have seen many 3D models ruined because of a poor light setup. As a result, you end up with a scene that has an okay-looking model and bad lighting. Needless to say, when showcasing your work, this is not what you want.

Standard Light Types in 3D Studio MAX

By default, when you open up Max and start working, it has its own default lights set up. If it didn't, everything would be pitch black. These default lights are not actual selectable lights; it is a built-in system that allows you to see what you're doing. By default, when you create a light in 3ds Max, this system is turned off. So oftentimes you add a single light to a scene and you think, "Wow, it's suddenly dark." That's because now you only have one light source in your world.

Alright, let's get to it. First of all, there are way too many ways to create lighting inside of 3D Studio MAX to go into all of them in detail. Lighting is an art all to itself. In fact, just as you are reading this book to get a better understanding of 3D Studio MAX, you could go out and get an entire book on lighting. However, I can get you started and give you the tools needed to create beautiful scenes and showcase your work properly.

Let's first start off by showing you where to access your main lights. Go to the Create panel and select the Light button.

Figure 5-1: The Light button.

You will see a group of buttons that let you select the six different standard light types available. Let's run down the differences between these lights.

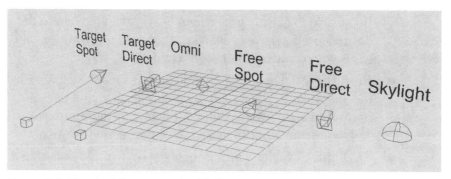

Figure 5-2: The six different standard lights.

- **Target Spot:** The Target Spot light is just that; it's a light with a target attached to it. The light starts as a small point and fades outward the farther away it gets from its source. The target is where the light is pointed. Think of a theater spotlight used to follow an actor around on stage. There is a point of origin and a target. Your light source will always look at (or face) your target.

- **Target Direct:** A Target Direct light works the same as a Target Spot. The only difference is that a Target Direct light emits light from an area and does not fade outward. It shoots a focused beam of light that will not "cone" out the farther away it gets from the camera.

- **Omni:** The Omni light casts light in all directions. Think of a lamp without its shade. Without the shade to focus the light in specific directions, the light is cast in all directions evenly. The Omni light is very powerful and is a great way to fill a room with light or create specific pools of light and shadow.

- **Free Spot:** The Free Spot is the same as the Target Spot, minus the target. In order to make a Free Spot light (or any light without a target) face an object, you have to rotate it. In almost every case it is easier to just use the Target Spot. Being able to quickly grab a light's target and move it to the desired location is very efficient. However, there are certain cases where you may not want a target.

- **Free Direct:** The Free Direct light performs the same as the Target Direct light. Its only difference is that it does not have a target. Thus, to point your light, you have to move and rotate it in order to make it face the desired location.

- **Skylight:** Skylight is meant to model daylight. It gives you a very accurate representation of ambient shadow and light cover. You don't, however, receive any specular highlights from a skylight. You must use it in conjunction with an additional light if you want to achieve a highlight on your object.

The remaining lights in your light list are Mental Ray lights (as indicated by the "mr" before them). These lights require you to use the Mental Ray renderer, which is not covered in this book in depth; thus I will let you explore those on your own.

Creating a Light

Creating a light is very simple. If it is a "target" light, then you must place your cursor at the desired origin of the light. Hold the left mouse button and drag until your cursor is where you want your target, then release the left-click. This will create your origin and your target. If it is a light type without a target (such as an Omni light), then simply left-click once in the desired location.

Create a Target light in your Top viewport.

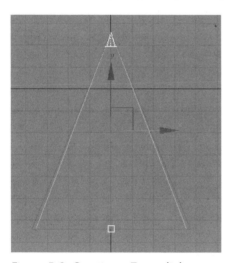

Figure 5-3: Creating a Target light.

Now in your Perspective viewport, grab the light and move it upward.

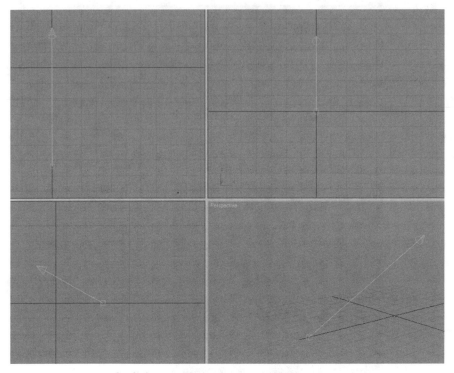

Figure 5-4: Moving the light source.

You'll notice the target stayed in its place but the light source moved. Now grab the target and move it around a bit. You can see the light source following its target.

By the way, you have no idea how helpful it is to be able to create a light and its target anywhere you want in the scene. It probably seems very logical to you; however, if you were using other packages like Maya or even XSI, you would not be so lucky. In those environments all creation starts at zero, which means you have to create your light and its target at zero before moving them to the desired location. With Max, you make the light and its target in the desired location first. This is a much faster way to work.

Understanding the Light Settings

Create a Target Spot anywhere in your viewports. Make sure the light is selected, and then open up your Modify panel to the right. You'll notice you have a whole mess of rollouts available to you!

Figure 5-5: The Modify panel for a Target Spot.

Let's run through the basic settings so you know what most of these things do.

General Parameters

By default, the General Parameters rollout should be open.

*Figure 5-6: The
General Parameters
rollout.*

In it you have a couple of check boxes and drop-down lists.
You can turn your light on and off quickly via a check box.

Next to the On check box is a drop-down list for the light
type.

*Figure 5-7: Choose
the light type here.*

This list allows you to actually change the kind of light you are
using on the fly. This means you can create a light and position
it in your scene; then if at any point you decide you need to
use a different type of light, you can simply toggle it using the
rollout. You don't need to delete your light and reposition a
new one and try to match your settings, etc. Just adjust the
rollout and the light will be changed and will keep your settings from the previous light.

You also have a check box to turn shadows on and off.

Figure 5-8: Turn
shadows on here.

By default, your lights will have this box unchecked. You may
wonder, Why would I ever not want my shadows turned on?
Well, you will notice very quickly that having shadows on can
increase your render times dramatically. You may not want to
turn on all your shadows until you are ready to view a final
render.

Under the Shadows check boxes you have another
drop-down that reads Shadow Map. This drop-down list allows
you to change your shadow type.

Figure 5-9: Choose
the shadow type
here.

By default, all lights in Max use what is called a shadow map
to create their shadows. In order to not overcomplicate things,
I want you to stick with the Shadow Map setting for right now.

Intensity/Color/Attenuation

*Figure 5-10: The
Intensity/Color/
Attenuation rollout.*

The Intensity/Color/Attenuation rollout lets you change light
intensity, light color, and light attenuation, or "falloff." At the
top you have the Multiplier setting. The multiplier is the
light's power or brightness. You can change the Multiplier setting to a negative number to actually remove light from an
area (not many people are aware of that). You can also raise
the Multiplier setting into the thousands, although after about
5.0 it basically just shoots a completely solid white light that
floods anything it hits.

Next to the Multiplier setting you have a color swatch.
This color swatch represents the light color. Double-clicking
on that color swatch will bring up a color selector. You can
then choose any color you want for the light.

Let's drop down a bit now to the Near Attenuation and Far Attenuation groups.

Figure 5-11: The Near Attenuation and Far Attenuation settings.

Light attenuation is a fancy way of saying that light loses its energy the farther away from its source it gets. For example, if you take a flashlight and shine it onto the ground, you'll notice that the light fades off into the distance. Max gives you Near Attenuation and Far Attenuation settings to manually adjust your light's "fade." By default, your Max lights have attenuation turned off. Like the Shadows setting, this is for faster render times. To use light attenuation you need to make sure the Use check box is checked. The Show check box gives you a visual representation of your light's actual attenuation. You will need to check this box in order to see how your light will be attenuated. After activating your light's attenuation, by default it should look like Figure 5-12.

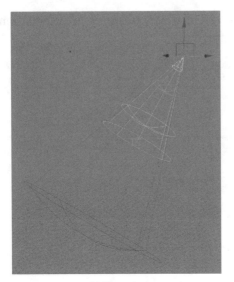

Figure 5-12: A light with attenuation on.

If you want to modify the default attenuation settings, you can do so using the arrows to the right. As with most spinners in Max, you can adjust them with your mouse and watch the attenuation update in your viewport.

Spotlight Parameters

*Figure 5-13: The
Spotlight Parameters
rollout.*

There are two check boxes at the top of the Spotlight Parameters rollout: Show Cone and Overshoot. Turning on Show Cone makes the light's cone visible even when it is not selected. Turning on Overshoot makes your light shoot light outward past the area of its cone. This is useful when shooting very large outside scenes. For example, when shooting an outdoor scene you need your entire scene to receive light. You may not, however, want your light to cast shadows on the entire scene. For this, you would set your light cone to the area you wish to receive shadow, then turn on Overshoot. This will light everything under your light, but only cast shadow in the area that falls within your light cone.

Below the check boxes you have the Hotspot/Beam and Falloff/Field settings. Your light's hotspot is the brightest part of the light. The falloff is the distance from the hotspot to the edge of the light's cone.

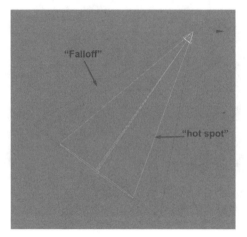

Figure 5-14: A light's hotspot and falloff areas.

By default, Max lights use a cone or circular light. You can, however, change that to a square light (similar to a fluorescent ceiling light in an office). You can change your light from a circular light to a rectangular light by choosing the Rectangle option.

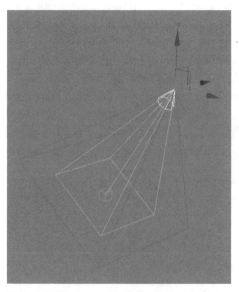

Figure 5-15: A square light.

If you want to adjust the light's aspect ratio, simply use the Aspect spinner.

Advanced Effects

Figure 5-16: The Advanced Effects rollout.

The Advanced Effects rollout is a quick way to make tweaks to your light settings. For example, after getting a light set up the way you want it, you may still find you want to adjust the light's contrast. You may also want to adjust your shadow's edge softness. You can do both very quickly and easily with the Advanced Effects rollout settings. You can even turn off a light's ability to cast a specular highlight by unchecking the Specular option. This means that your light will cast an even distribution of light across an object without creating a hotspot.

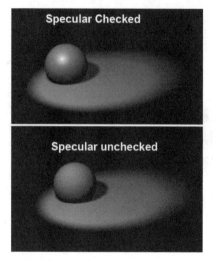

Figure 5-17: Sphere with and without specular light.

Another neat trick is the Projector Map option. The best way to explain a projection map is to think of the old *Batman* shows. Remember when they used to shine the Batman symbol into the air when they needed Batman? That's an example of a projection map. You are basically placing an image over your light in order for it to cast a specific shadow. It can be something very obvious like the Batman symbol, or it can be something more subtle like faking water caustics being cast onto a wall near an indoor pool. If you want to use a projector map, you must first pick the map you want. By default, the Map slot is empty.

Figure 5-18: Choose a projector map here.

To place an image in the Projector Map slot, press the button to the right of the Map check box. This will bring up the Material/Map browser. Select Bitmap in the browser, then find any image (black and white preferred) and press Open. After selecting the desired bitmap, make sure that the check box to the left of your map slot is checked. The check box allows you to toggle whether or not the light is used as a projector.

Shadow Parameters

*Figure 5-19: The
Shadow Parameters
rollout.*

The only part of the Shadow Parameters rollout I want you to worry about is the shadow Color and Density settings.

You can adjust your light's shadow color using the Color swatch. You can also adjust your light's shadow density with the Density spinner. By default, the shadow density for all lights is set to 1.0. At 1.0 the shadow is solid black. The closer to 0.0 you get, the lighter the shadow becomes.

Shadow Map Parameters

The Shadow Map Parameters rollout contains your base shadow settings. You have three spinners that will set the tone for the look of your shadow: Bias, Size, and Sample Range.

Figure 5-20: The Shadow Map Parameters rollout.

The shadow bias is the distance between an object and the start of its shadow.

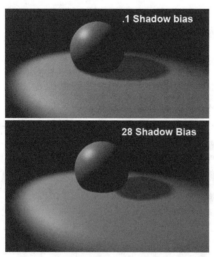

Figure 5-21: A higher setting for Bias makes the object look like it is floating above its shadow.

Next to the Bias setting is the Size setting. The shadow size is the number of subdivisions (or resolution) for the map that is creating the shadow. The greater the value, the more detailed the map will be. Think of it as increasing your shadow density or quality. I have no official proof of this, but I have heard that Max processes values faster if you keep the shadow sizes in 2's (256 x 2 = 512, 512 x 2 = 1024, and so on).

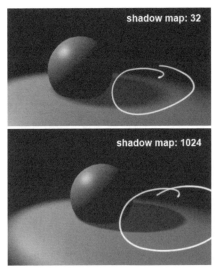

Figure 5-22: Increasing the Size setting sharpens the shadow's edges.

Last but not least is the Sample Range setting. The sample range determines how much the different areas within the shadow are averaged. This basically means it will determine how smooth the edge of the shadow is.

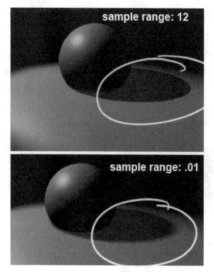

Figure 5-23: The Sample Range setting averages the areas of the shadow map. Higher settings smooth the edges.

The remaining rollouts pertain to atmosphere effects and the Mental Ray renderer. If you start venturing into the sections we've discussed, then you'll learn your way around the light settings pretty quickly.

Chapter 6

Rendering Your Scene

Understanding What Rendering Is

What exactly is rendering? Well, rendering compiles all the information in your scene. It takes all your shaders, lighting, models, effects, and everything you have created and makes your final image or animation. When you watch *Finding Nemo* or *The Incredibles*, you are watching a final render. It's got all the bells and whistles.

Using the Default Renderer

Max has two renderers: the default renderer and the Mental Ray renderer. By default, you will be using Max's default scanline renderer. Get comfortable with it and know it well; it is very powerful and can do most anything. In fact, all rendered images you see in this book were created using the default renderer. I would recommend, however, after you have gotten your feet wet in Max's default renderer, you may want to eventually try rendering using the Mental Ray renderer. Mental Ray is a general-purpose renderer that can generate physically correct simulations of lighting effects, including ray-traced reflections and refractions, caustics, and global illumination.

The Render Scene Dialog Box

Let's take a look at the Render Scene dialog. Press the Render Scene Dialog button in the upper right-hand side of your user interface.

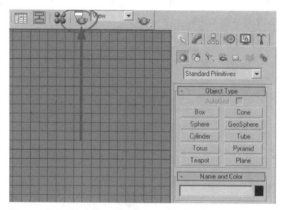

Figure 6-1: The Render Scene Dialog button.

This will bring up the Render Scene dialog box.

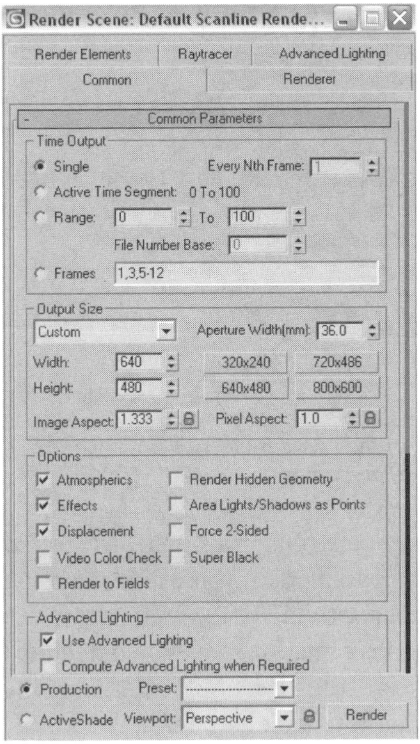

Figure 6-2: The Render Scene dialog.

I know, I know, lots of scary numbers and buttons. It's not nearly as complicated as you think though. At the top is the Common Parameters rollout, which houses almost 100 percent of your default rendering options. At the top of the rollout is the Time Output group.

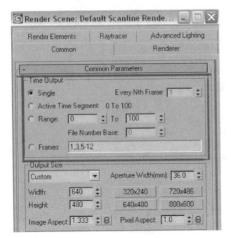

Figure 6-3: The Time Output group contains settings for frame number(s) and frequency, range, and more.

By default, Max will only render a single picture; however, if you are rendering an animation, you would need to tell Max what range to render within. For example, if you needed to render a 2,000-frame animation, you would need to first activate the Range option, then type in the desired range. In that case you would want it to look like this:

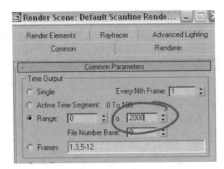

Figure 6-4: For an animation, choose a range of frames.

Below the Range setting is the Frames setting. This is a nice feature that lets you render out specific frame numbers. If, for example, you rendered out your animation and noticed a few rendering issues on some frames, you could tell Max to render out those specific frames, even though they don't fall one after another.

Below the Time Output group is the Output Size group.

Figure 6-5: The Output Size group.

The Output Size settings simply tell Max how large or small you want your image to be rendered. By default, Width is set to 640 pixels and Height is set to 480 pixels. Max has four pre-set output sizes already set up for you.

Underneath the Output Size group is the Options group.

Figure 6-6: The Options group.

This is nothing more than a series of check boxes to turn on or off the desired effect. By default, the first three options should be checked. The only one you'll probably want to mess with is the Render to Fields check box. This tells Max to ren-der its images into even and odd fields. You would want to do this if you are rendering something that will be shown on television.

Next are the Advanced Lighting and Render Output groups.

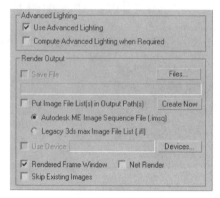

Figure 6-7: The Advanced Lighting and Render Output groups.

By default, the Use Advanced Lighting check box is checked. If you want to speed up your render times in order to preview them, you can uncheck this box to disable all advanced lighting.

The Render Output group allows you to save your animation or image automatically after it's finished rendering. You can save out multiple file types, or tell Max to render individual frames and save them one at a time automatically. To activate the Save File check box, you must first press the Files button.

Figure 6-8: Press the Files button and choose a file type and name.

Choose the designated file type and name of your file and press OK.

After all your settings are complete, you simply press the Render button at the bottom right of the Render Scene dialog.

Viewing the Safe Frame

The *safe frame* is the actual area of your screen that your camera will render. Your Perspective viewport is, for the most part, a square. But if you are rendering out a widescreen animation or image, you would get an incorrect representation of your camera's view. This is why you turn on Show Safe Frame.

To activate Show Safe Frame, right-click the viewport name to display a context menu.

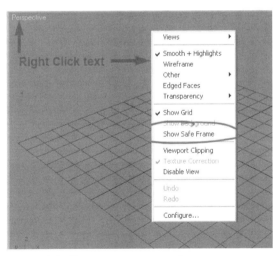

Figure 6-9: This menu pops up when you right-click the viewport name.

The Show Safe Frame command is halfway down. Left-click it to activate your safe frame display. The outermost yellow line on the screen now represents your actual camera view.

Anything outside of that yellow line will *not* show up in your render. The safe frame will update instantly whenever you change your aspect ratio or rendering output size.

Changing from the Default Renderer to the Mental Ray Renderer

After you feel comfortable with rendering, you may want to venture off into the land of the Mental Ray renderer. I am not going to go into Mental Ray here; that would take thousands of pages all by itself. I will simply show you how you change from the default scanline renderer to the Mental Ray renderer.

Open the Render Scene dialog again. At the very bottom is a rollout labeled Assign Renderer.

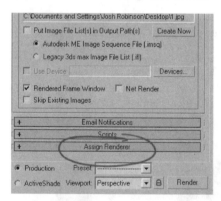

Figure 6-10: Open the Assign Renderer rollout at the bottom of the Render Scene dialog.

After you open up the Assign Renderer rollout, you'll see a list of options. The box next to Production reads Default Scanline Renderer. Press the Browse button to the right.

Figure 6-11: Press the Browse button next to Default Scanline Renderer to choose a new renderer.

A new window pops up that allows you to choose a renderer. Select the Mental Ray renderer. Done! You will now be rendering using Mental Ray. Also note that if you ever use any other third-party renderers such as Brasil or V-Ray, this is where you would choose those renderers too.

Chapter 7

Additional Modeling Tools and Modifiers

Sometimes the fastest way to create an object isn't to actually create it from scratch. In fact, if you can ever avoid doing so, you should. I very often work with industry professionals who reinvent the wheel many times over. My advice is to use the tools given to you to increase your workflow. Use the package to take as many shortcuts as you can. That's what it is there for. To accomplish this, Max has a host of modifiers that you can use to increase your workflow when modeling.

Lathe

The Lathe modifier is a slick way to create complicated circular objects. An example of this would be a building pillar, a candlestick, or even a detailed car tire.

Figure 7-1: Complicated circular objects can be created quickly with the Lathe modifier.

The Lathe modifier works by wrapping a spline shape that you create around a designated axis.

Let's make a quick candlestick to show you just how it works. First of all, when you are using the Lathe tool, you need to think in "halves." If this is your candlestick:

Figure 7-2: The completed candlestick.

then you need to draw out *half* of that object's profile. Think of it as cutting the object in half and then tracing what you have left with a spline. With this shape in mind, let's recreate it using a spline.

In the Create panel, select Shapes and then select the Line tool.

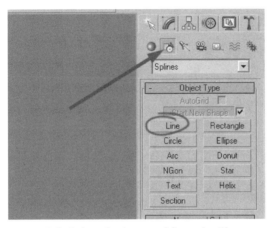

Figure 7-3: Select the Line tool from the Shapes panel.

Now, using the Line tool, trace the desired shape in your Front viewport. Every click you make will place a vertex. Don't be too worried about the shape being exact at first. We will go back and make all the necessary adjustments to it after we get the basic shape. After tracing our candlestick half, you should end up with something similar to Figure 7-4.

Now that we have our base vertices laid out we will need to modify them to get our exact shape.

Figure 7-4: Half of the candlestick has been traced.

Every vertex of a spline has the option of being one of four types of corners: Bezier Corner, Bezier, Smooth, or Corner. Each one has its own purpose.

To change a vertex to the desired corner type, first select the appropriate vertex and right-click. This will bring up your quad menus. In the upper-left quad, you'll notice you can change the selected vertex to one of the four corner types.

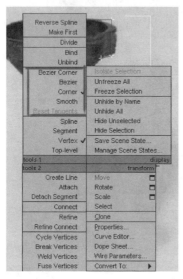

Figure 7-5: Right-click a vertex to display the quad menu.

Select all the vertices we created (they should now be high-lighted in red) and make all of these vertices Bezier. You'll notice now that every vertex has a pair of handles.

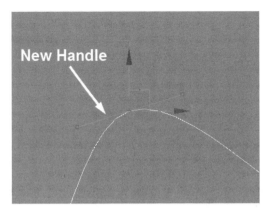

Figure 7-6: A Bezier vertex has two handles.

Each of those handles can be manipulated to create complex curved shapes, even without adding more vertices.

If you reselect all the vertices and change them all to be Corner, you'll notice that you get hard edges throughout the entire spline.

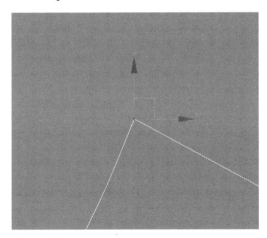

Figure 7-7: A Corner vertex.

Changing your vertex to Smooth will have the opposite effect. Smooth automatically averages out your curve for you.

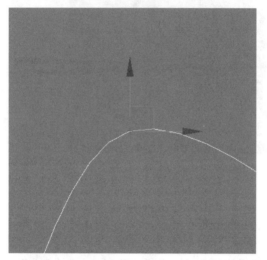

Figure 7-8: A Smooth vertex.

This is a quick way to create smooth curved shapes. It has fewer controls than one with Bezier curves, but it is faster.

Lastly, you have the Bezier Corner type. This type of vertex gives you the best of both worlds. You get the same handles that you get with a normal Bezier curve, but you can adjust each handle independently of the other.

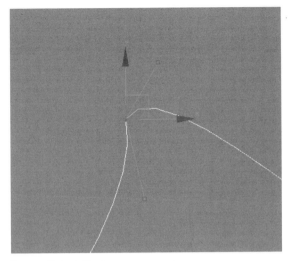

Figure 7-9: A Bezier corner vertex.

Reselect all your vertices and make them Bezier Corner vertices. Just experiment for a moment. Grab a couple of handles and move them around a bit. You'll notice how with Bezier Corners you can make sharp corners or round edges. This is the versatility of the Bezier Corner option.

With all this newfound knowledge in mind, go back to your spline and add all the subtle details that make up the profile of your candlestick. When you are done, it should look something like Figure 7-10.

Figure 7-10:
Your candlestick
half should look
like this.

Now that you have the world's most perfect spline, let's go ahead and add the Lathe modifier onto it. Access the Lathe modifier in the Modifiers rollout. (The Modifiers rollout is arranged alphabetically.) You'll notice that your shape immediately blows up into some weird round shape.

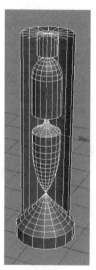

Figure 7-11:
The candlestick
with the Lathe
modifier
applied.

Let's just adjust the axis really quick to make sure that we are getting the correct shape. In your modifier stack, you'll notice a small plus sign (+) next to the Lathe modifier. Pressing the plus sign opens up the Lathe modifier's axis settings. You now have control over the lathe's axis point. Go back to the Front view and move the axis to the left or right until you see the lathe reacting properly and creating your candlestick shape for you (should be to the left, I believe). Cool, huh? You should have a pretty nifty-looking candlestick now.

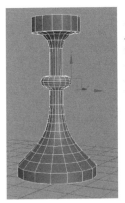

Figure 7-12: After you move the axis left, the candlestick should look like this.

The Lathe modifier also has a few settings.

Figure 7-13: The Lathe modifier settings.

Most notably, you can adjust the degrees that the lathe will travel as well as the number of segments it takes to get there.

Taper

The Taper modifier produces a tapered contour by scaling one or both ends of an object up or down. You can very easily control the amount of taper or curve using the spinners in the Taper modifier.

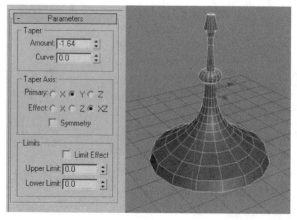

Figure 7-14: The Taper modifier settings.

You can even limit the amount of taper to a section of your object.

Like most other objects, you can adjust your taper at the sub-object level by opening up the stack.

Figure 7-15: Open the stack to apply the taper at the sub-object level.

You can manipulate the gizmo that is controlling your taper settings to create even more custom tapers and effects. Create your own object and use the Taper modifier to come up with your own unique shapes.

Bend

The Bend modifier lets you bend your object around a single axis. It creates a perfectly even bend across an object's geometry. You can bend that object on any of the three axes. Just like the Taper modifier, you can limit the bend to only affect a portion of the geometry.

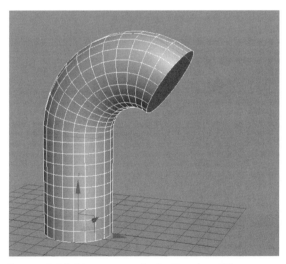

Figure 7-16: You can apply the Bend modifier to a specific section of an object.

To bend any object you must first have enough segments in order to bend it. If you don't have any segments, you cannot bend anything! This may sound obvious, but I can't tell you how many times in the very beginning I tried to use some of these tools and thought they didn't work! Look, I was born in a small town. Cut me some slack, okay?

After applying a bend to an object, you have settings similar to the Taper modifier. You can adjust your object's bend angle and manually adjust its direction. You can also quickly cycle through your three axes to determine what axis it is bending around.

Also, as with many geometry modifiers, you can use the Limits settings to apply the bend to a specific part of the geometry. And, like Taper, you can adjust your bend at the sub-object level.

Twist

The Twist modifier creates a twirling or spinning effect across an object's geometry.

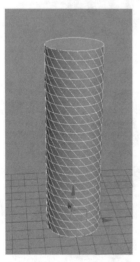

Figure 7-17: A cylinder with a Twist modifier applied.

You can control the angle of the twist on any of the three axes as well as limit the twist to a specific area of the geometry.

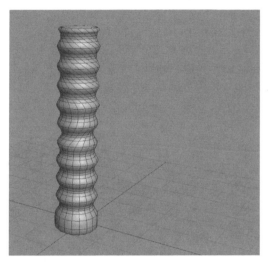

Figure 7-18: This twist starts at the center of the cylinder because of the limits that were set.

To twist an object, first select the object and apply the Twist modifier. The Parameters rollout allows you to set the Twist Axis to X, Y, or Z. You can set the angle of the twist using the Angle spinner provided. You can also use the Bias spinner to "bunch up" your twists at either side of the object. Last, you can adjust the twist at its sub-object level and manipulate the actual twist gizmo to further manipulate your twist.

TurboSmooth

TurboSmooth was introduced in Max 7.0 to replace the original MeshSmooth modifier. TurboSmooth simply uses a much more efficient algorithm and performs much better than MeshSmooth.

TurboSmooth takes your model and smoothes everything out for you.

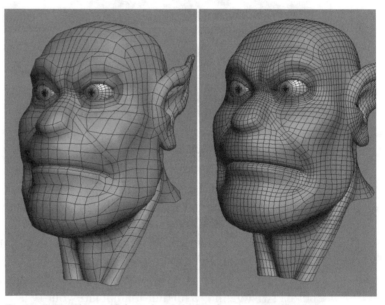

Figure 7-19: The model on the right has been smoothed with TurboSmooth.

You see these very detailed models online and in movies. No one actually models all those little lines, etc.; they create a less detailed model and then smooth it. Let the computer work *for* you. You create your base model and you create detail where you want it. Then you apply TurboSmooth to smooth out your model. You can also set the interpolation level, which means that you control how smooth and how dense you want your geometry to become.

The best way to use TurboSmooth is at the sub-object level. Apply TurboSmooth to an Edit Poly object. Your stack should look like this:

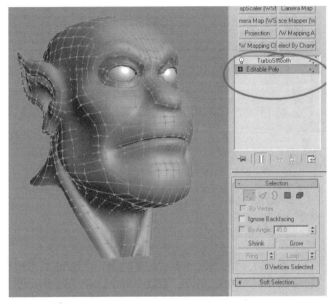

Figure 7-20: The Edit Poly stack after applying TurboSmooth.

By default, your iterations are set to 1.0. The great thing about TurboSmooth is that you can really up the iteration level without slowing down your viewport. In the past, keeping your iteration level at 3 or 4 would really hit your video card pretty hard. But with the new TurboSmooth, you can work very quickly even at high iteration levels.

After applying TurboSmooth, go back down your stack and highlight Editable Poly.

Figure 7-21:
Highlight Editable
Poly.

Notice that your box pops back to its original shape before the TurboSmooth operation. That's because you are viewing that part of the stack. If you want to view the top result of your stack, even while working at the bottom of the stack, press the Show End Result button.

Figure 7-22: The
Show End Result
button.

This will allow you to work in Edit Poly mode while viewing your smoothed Edit Poly object! This is glorious! To see just how this works, make sure you are at the bottom of your stack and select Vertex mode. You'll notice an orange outline representing the bottom of your stack, even though you are viewing the top of it.

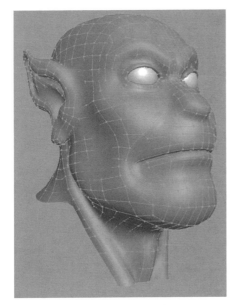

Figure 7-23: The orange outline represents the bottom of the stack.

You also have the option of toggling the Show End Result button if you want to work without viewing the top of your stack all the time.

Vertex Weighting and Edge Creasing

When you are using TurboSmooth you also get a couple of nifty little features located in the Edit Edges rollout, such as vertex weighting and edge creasing.

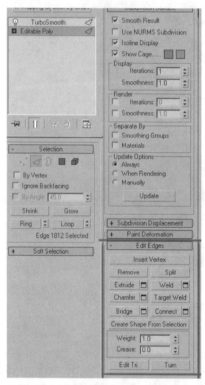

Figure 7-24: The Edit Edges rollout.

Create a box and collapse it to an Edit Poly object. Now apply TurboSmooth. Go to the bottom of your stack and choose Edge mode. Next, turn on your Show End Result button again. Select any edge and set the Crease level to 1.0. You'll notice that this creases your edge for you! This is a *great* feature. You just created a hard edge on a smooth object and you did it without adding polygons.

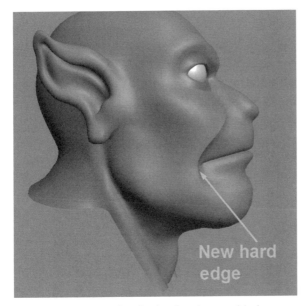

Figure 7-25: A new hard edge has been added.

Go to Vertex mode this time and look for the Weight option
located in the Edit Vertices rollout.

*Figure 7-26: The
Weight option.*

Select a vertex and increase your vertex weighting. You'll
notice the box begins to pull toward the weighted vertex.
Score! The use of vertex weighting and edge creasing can
allow you to quickly make difficult changes to your geometry.

Lofting

Welcome to the wonderful world of lofting! Loft objects are two-dimensional shapes (splines) extruded along a path that you designate.

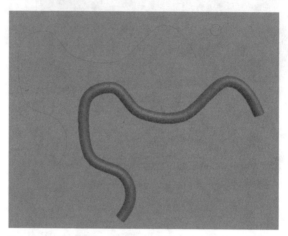

Figure 7-27: A lofted object.

Loft has many options and possibilities; however, the basic procedure is very easy.

One method is to create a loft via Get Shape. First, create a path. It can be any path that you create using the Line tool.

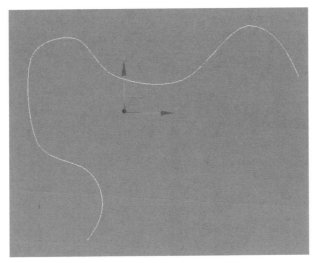

Figure 7-28: Create a path with the Line tool.

Next, you need to draw the shape that you want to send on the "path." In this case we'll just use a spline circle.

Figure 7-29: Create a shape to send on your path.

Next, select your "path" or road and then choose Create> Compound>Loft from the main menu.

Figure 7-30: Choose the Loft command.

In the Creation Method rollout, click the Get Shape button.

Figure 7-31: Click the Get Shape button.

Done. You just created a Loft object!

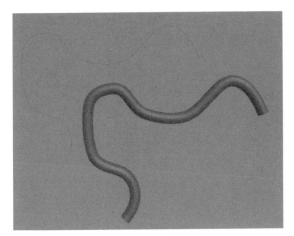

Figure 7-32: The completed Loft object.

There are several settings for you to play around with. I recommend experimenting a bit. Pay close attention, however, to the Skin Parameters rollout. This is where you can add or remove detail automatically using the Shape Steps and Path Steps settings.

Chapter 8

Architectural Modeling Exercise: Interior

Creating a Floor Plan

Let me first just say before we get going that I am a total idiot. I got about 70 percent of the way through this chapter before I realized I was doing it all wrong! I originally laid out the interior using splines. Using splines is a really good generic way to teach someone to create interiors and, if you are using competing packages like Maya, you would have no choice, but we are not. Let's go ahead and use Max's "wall" generator instead and save ourselves major amounts of time.

Let's get started! Since we are going to create our walls using Max's wall generator, we don't need to worry about wall thickness in the beginning. That is something we will set up using the Outline tool after we get our walls laid out.

Before we get started you will need to activate your snap tools. To do this, simply press the Snap icon to activate your snaps.

Figure 8-1: Activate Snap.

In Max you have many snap options. To access those options, right-click on the Snaps icon. This will display a dialog called Grid and Snap Settings.

Figure 8-2: The Grid and Snap Settings dialog.

The Snaps tab contains 12 check box options. Checking a box means that your cursor will snap to that object. You can snap to multiple objects at the same time. This is a huge feature. You can simultaneously snap to your grid, an edge, a midpoint, etc. This is such a huge asset when doing architectural modeling and will speed up your creation process dramatically. For what we are doing, we will need to check the Grid Points check box. This will snap your cursor to the floor grid.

Let me first explain the wall generator a bit. The wall works very quickly because you lay it out like a spline. The difference is that it has adjustable height and width settings. Moreover, because your wall is created procedurally, it is completely unwrapped for you. (You can even explore the sub-object settings a bit to reveal many other options.) However, we'll only be creating the walls and then setting a height and width here.

To access the wall generator, make sure you have the Geometry button pressed in the Create panel.

Figure 8-3: Click the Geometry button.

By default, the drop-down list below the Geometry button should read Standard Primitives. We want to open up that list and select AEC Extended.

Figure 8-4: Choose AEC Extended from the drop-down list.

After selecting AEC Extended, you'll see a few new options pop up, including Foliage, Wall, and Railing. Max has the unique ability to create many things on the fly. These are just a few. If you were using any other 3D package you'd be manually creating these walls, railings, windows, and doors and then unwrapping them all piece by piece. Brutal! We are very lucky to have these options available in Max.

Make sure that your 3D snaps are activated and set to Grid Points. Now maximize the Top viewport. This is the view where we'll be creating our basic layout. Press the Wall button in the Object Type list to activate the wall generator. Before you actually start creating the wall, set your wall height and width. Since we are using generic Max units right now, just set Width to 3.5 and Height to 45.0.

Figure 8-5: Set the width and height before you create the wall.

 Note:

You can change your Max units to read Feet and Inches by selecting Units Setup from the Customize menu.

Now that we have our width and height set, we can create the outer walls. Using your grid snaps, recreate the shape that I have laid out in Figure 8-6.

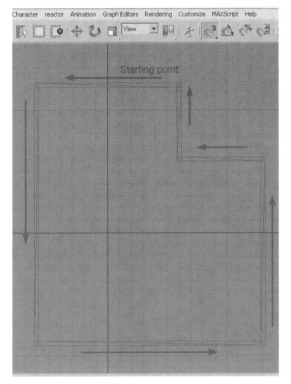

Figure 8-6: Create the outer walls.

Don't be too worried about getting the exact distances from one corner to another. Just recreate the shape as best you can. After you connect the last wall, Max will ask if you want to weld points. Click Yes. This will close off our wall. After selecting Yes, right-click to stop using the Wall tool.

Now that the outer wall is complete, we need to create our inner walls. Our inner walls will define the halls and rooms.

Using the same technique, create the three inner walls I have laid out in Figure 8-7.

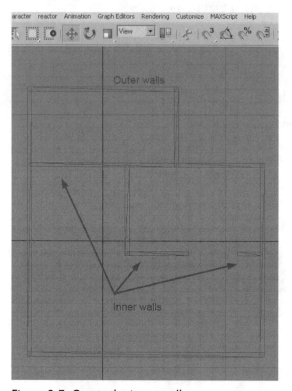

Figure 8-7: Create the inner walls.

 Note:

The Wall tool remembers your last height and width settings, so your new walls will be created with the same settings as the outer walls.

You are completely done with the wall layout process at this point. Your Perspective viewport should look something like this:

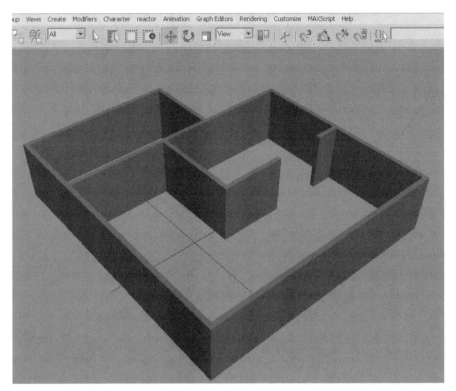

Figure 8-8: The wall setup in the Perspective viewport.

Adding Windows and Doorways

Before we create any detail trim, we need to make sure we have all our doors and windows laid out. As you can see, we have one room that is totally closed off at the moment. I actually did this on purpose so that I could show you a nifty way to quickly create doorways. We are going to create what is called a Boolean. A Boolean operation can do several things; in this case, however, we are going to create a Boolean in order to punch a hole into our wall to create our door opening.

The first thing we need to do is create an object to punch the hole. Obviously, this object should be in the shape of a door. Create a box and place it through the wall at the doorway location.

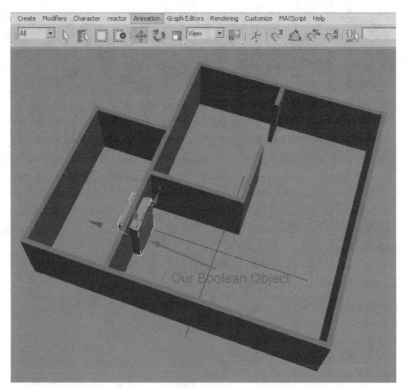

Figure 8-9: Place a box in the doorway.

Note:

You must place your Boolean object all the way through the wall. If you do not, then it will not punch a hole all the way through. The Boolean object will remove everything that it is intersecting.

To access the Boolean feature, first select the correct wall. Then choose Create>Compound>Boolean from the menu bar.

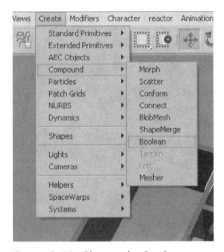

Figure 8-10: Choose the Boolean command.

Upon doing this, the modification window to the right should have changed and you should see all the Boolean options now. Most importantly, there is a large button just below the layer stack that reads Pick Operand B.

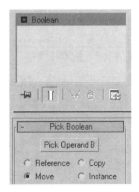

Figure 8-11: The Pick Operand B button.

Double-check to make sure you still have the correct wall selected. Now press the Pick Operand B button. It should be highlighted in yellow once it's pressed. Now go into the Perspective viewport and select the box that we are using to punch the hole (that box is our Operand B). Kerplow! The box you selected should have disappeared and a hole should remain.

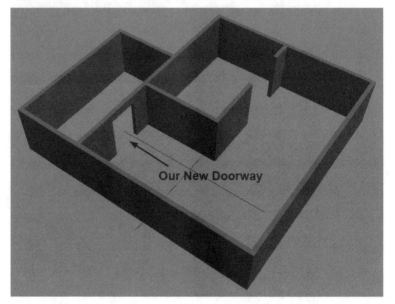

Figure 8-12: The box has disappeared and the hole remains.

Let's repeat the same process to create a window.

 Note:

As a rule, after I perform a Boolean operation on an object, I collapse it to an Editable Poly (or mesh) object before performing a second Boolean operation.

So let's repeat the Boolean process one more time to create a window. Create a Boolean object, select the wall you wish to break, and then select the Boolean object.

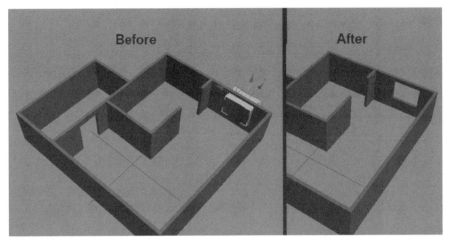

Figure 8-13: Creating a window with a Boolean.

Creating Trim Detail Around the Bottom of the Walls

Just to add a bit of detail, I want to create a basic floor trim that we can run along the bottom of our walls. There are two basic ways to create floor trim: You can create a loft, or you can outline a spline and extrude it upward. The only reason you would ever need to create a loft would be if you had a very detailed and specific shape for your trim. Since the point of this exercise is not to create the world's greatest trim, we will use the spline technique (which will look fine).

✎ **Note:**

Make sure that all the walls you created are flush with their connecting walls. This is just a precaution because I can't see what you have made so far; however, all your walls should be flush against each other.

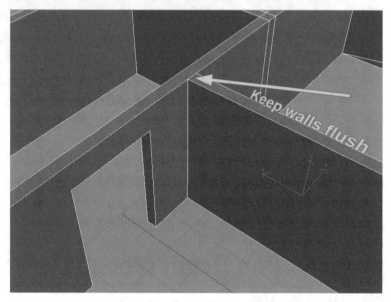

Figure 8-14: Ensure that all walls are flush.

The first thing that we need to do is trace our entire interior using a spline. Adjust your snap settings so that they are set to snap on Endpoint as shown in Figure 8-15.

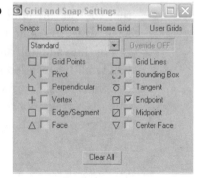

Figure 8-15: Set the snaps to Endpoint.

Now using the Line tool (Create panel>Shapes>Line), snap a line around the entire interior. The goal is to have a single spline that traces the interior floor. You can do this in Perspective view if you want. If you do, however, you will most likely have to create a spline, then rotate around your view a bit, create another spline, rotate again, and so on. In the end you will end up with several splines that you will need to attach to each other and weld together. You can do this very quickly of course, but I'll use this as an opportunity to show you a neat trick using Max's 2.5-dimensional snapping. Using this technique will make this process faster and also create a single spline from the beginning.

To activate your 2.5-dimensional snapping, hold the left-click on the Snap button to display a drop-down containing a few options.

Figure 8-16: The Snap drop-down.

Select the button that says 2.5. You have now activated the 2.5-D snapping. All 2.5 does is allow you to snap on the ground plane. It basically lets you use the full strength of your snaps without including the Z axis.

Maximize the Top view and begin tracing the interior walls. Max will ask you if you want to close your spline after you connect it to itself on the last vertex. You *do* want to close the spline; if you didn't, then the spline would not be welded closed. When complete, you should have a shape that conforms to the interior and looks something like Figure 8-17.

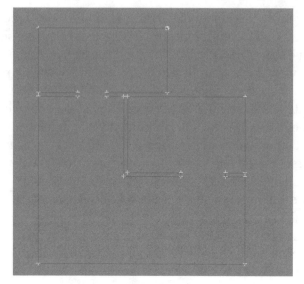

Figure 8-17: The completed spline.

I also raised the final spline up off the ground in our Perspective view a bit just so you can see exactly what we have created.

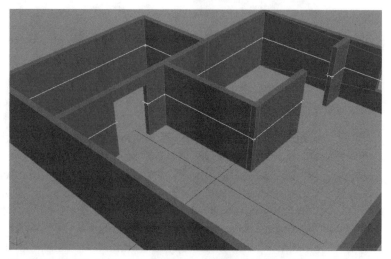

Figure 8-18: The completed spline has been raised a bit.

Let's create our spline outline now. Select the Spline sub-object.

Figure 8-19: Select the Spline sub-object under Selection.

Now select all spline segments within your Perspective viewport. They should be highlighted in red. Return to the Modify panel and scroll down until you find the Outline button.

Figure 8-20: The Outline button.

Pressing the Outline button returns you to the Perspective viewport and manually outlines the spline. Considering how small and precise our outline will be, let's just go ahead and type it in manually in the provided slot. The larger the number, the larger the outline. I used .5 for my outline. If you take a closer look now at your spline, you should notice that you've created a spline border around your entire interior.

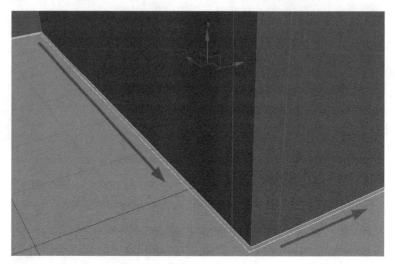

Figure 8-21: The outlined spline.

Exit sub-object mode and apply an Extrude modifier on top of your spline. Applying an Extrude will raise the spline off the ground plane and transform it into geometry at the same time. After applying the Extrude, you need to set a height. I chose to go with a height of 4.0. You could make this higher or lower, of course. After applying these settings, your trim detail should look like Figure 8-22.

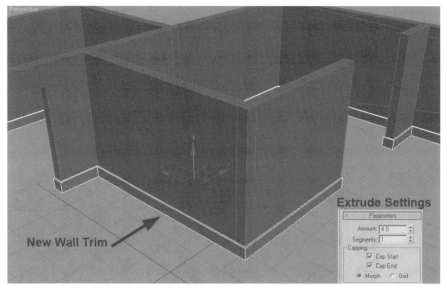

Figure 8-22: The completed floor trim.

Congratulations! You have successfully created the floor trim!

Creating the Floor and Ceiling Plane

We are going to actually use the trim piece to create our floor and ceiling. First, select the trim and copy it (hold Shift and select the trim). Now, in the modifier stack, I want you to get rid of the Extrude modifier we applied earlier. This will make the trim piece a spline again. Next, go into sub-object mode and get rid of the spline that was created when we performed the outline (that means get rid of the innermost spline). What should remain is the original spline that we created when making the floor trim.

Note:

Experience would teach you to just make a copy of the original spline you created and keep it for a backup because you would surely be needing it again.

Now that we have our original spline shape, I want you to apply an Extrude modifier to it. Keep your extrude settings at 0.0 since we don't actually need any height. When complete, the ground plane should be a perfect fit for the interior.

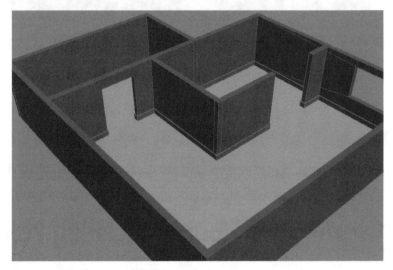

Figure 8-23: The completed ground plane.

To create the ceiling, all we need to do is copy the floor and move it up to the desired ceiling height. When you are done, your interior should look something like this:

Figure 8-24: The completed interior with floor and ceiling.

Creating a Basic Floor Texture with a Reflection

All I want to do in this last section is create a floor texture with a bit of reflection. You will be amazed at how quickly a scene like this can come to life, even without proper texturing. We are going to add a single color to the floor and apply a reflection.

Open up the Material Editor and apply a simple gray texture to all of the interior. Let's add just a bit of specular highlight and glossiness onto our gray texture just for good measure.

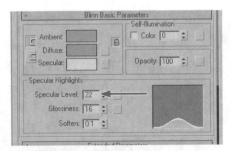

*Figure 8-25: Make the interior gray with
a bit of specular highlight and glossiness.*

Very few things absorb 100 percent of light. Even the slightest
bit of highlight usually makes a huge difference. Highlights
also add much more depth to your scene.

Now let's work on that floor texture. Select a new shader
and adjust the color to a burnt orange color with RGB settings
of 192, 105, 34.

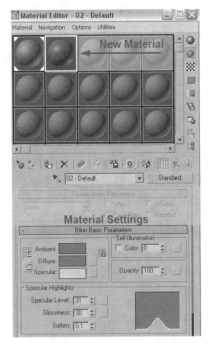

*Figure 8-26: Make the new shader
a burnt orange color.*

Now apply this new material to the floor. The scene should now look like this:

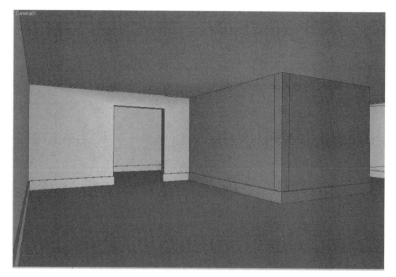

Figure 8-27: *The floor now has a burnt orange color and also a bit of specular and glossiness highlight.*

All we have left to do is apply a simple reflection to our floor. Expand the Maps rollout in your Material Editor and select the Reflection slot.

Figure 8-28: *Choose the Reflection map.*

This will open up a new window with a large number of material options. In most cases, you would select Bitmap and choose the appropriate bitmap, but in this case, we want to use the Flat Mirror option.

Figure 8-29: Choose the Flat Mirror material.

When it comes to creating a real reflection, most 3D packages will only give you the option to ray-trace a reflection. But we are not using just *any* package — we are using 3ds Max!

Ray tracing traces the path of rays sampled from the light source. Reflections and refractions generated this way are physically accurate. So that's great, right? Well, yeah it's great, but it's like shooting a mouse with a flame-thrower. Kind of an overkill for something as simple as a floor reflection. The Flat Mirror option will create a perfect reflection in about half the time, so we are going to use this as our method of reflection.

 Note:

Flat Mirror only works on perfectly flat surfaces.

After applying the Flat Mirror material to your reflection channel, you get a small list of options. In order to make the Flat Mirror work, you have to tell your material which face you want to be reflective. If you don't do this, then you won't see any reflection. Here, we don't want the bottom and sides of our floor geometry to reflect, only the top polygon. To designate which polygon you want to reflect, check the Apply to Faces with ID check box.

Figure 8-30: Choose the Apply to Faces with ID option.

By default, the ID given is 1. That means we need to make sure our top polygon is set to 1. To find out what our top polygon is, go into the sub-object mode of the floor and select the top polygon. Under Polygon Properties you'll see a material ID number.

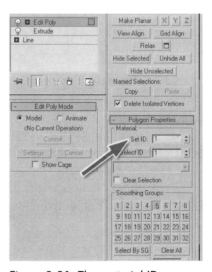

Figure 8-31: The material ID number.

It is most likely set to 1. If that is the case, then we are good to go! If not, be sure to change it to 1.

In your free time, explore a few of the other Flat Mirror settings. The Blur setting is especially helpful when creating a slightly blurred reflection. For what we are doing, however, we will just stick with all default settings.

Now let's back out and go to the parent level of our new material. You do this by hitting the Go To Parent button until you get to all your available slots.

Figure 8-32: The Go To Parent button.

By default, your Reflection setting is 100.

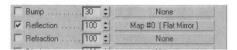

Figure 8-33: The Reflection setting is at 100.

That means you are reflecting 100 percent, which is a bit too much. Let's go ahead and make this about 25 or so. We are sooo done. All you need to do to see your reflection is do a quick render. So position your camera (if you have one) or your Perspective viewport and select Quick Render.

I put in just a few simple lights so you could see exactly what we built.

Figure 8-34: The completed room with a few simple lights.

Chapter 9

Organic Modeling Basics

Understanding the Concept of Box Modeling

The entire point of "box modeling" is that you work on a lower detail version of your model while the computer updates your actions on a high-detail version of the model in real time. (Or you can toggle back and forth between the low- and high-end models.)

When you pop in your favorite DVD and see all these crazy high-detail models, it's important to understand that those models are not created at that level of detail.

Don't get me wrong — you have to create a lot of detail! You may have to handcraft 40,000 polygons to get your character ready for smoothing, but then you smooth your model and increase the number of polygons. Sometimes two times more. Sometimes four times more. The T. rex in *Jurassic Park* had millions of polygons, and that was in the early '90s.

Computers are pushing more and more polygons every single year. The numbers coming out of the major studios now are getting pretty insane to say the least.

You don't always need millions and millions of polygons, though. You have to understand what your target goal is. If you are doing something for film, then you will need major polygon counts for it to hold its quality on such a large format. For example, an organic character or plant that has a tiny little edge that you can barely see on your computer monitor will be three feet wide on the big screen! The smallest errors on your computer screen will be ten times bigger once fully rendered for film.

The Difference between MeshSmooth and Max 7.0's TurboSmooth

TurboSmooth was introduced in Max 7.0 to replace the original MeshSmooth modifier. TurboSmooth simply uses a much more efficient algorithm and performs much better than the already efficient MeshSmooth. In fact, it's not uncommon to efficiently work on a model with a smooth iteration of 3 or 4 using TurboSmooth.

What MeshSmooth and TurboSmooth do is take your model and smooth everything out for you. Although you see these very detailed models online and in movies, no one actually models all those little lines. You create a less detailed model and then you smooth it. Let the computer work for you.

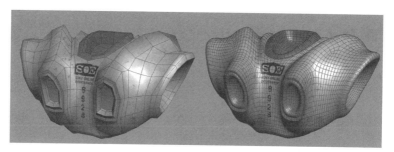

Figure 9-1: Original model at left and smoothed model at right.

You create your base model and then create detail where you want it. Then you apply TurboSmooth to smooth out your model. You also set the iteration level.

Figure 9-2: Set the number of iterations here.

This lets you control how smooth and how dense you want your geometry to become.

Stacking the TurboSmooth Modifier to See the End Result

The best way to use TurboSmooth is at the sub-object level. Apply a TurboSmooth to an Edit Poly object. Your stack should look like this:

Figure 9-3: Editable Poly in the Turbo-Smooth stack.

By default, your iterations are set to 1. The great thing about TurboSmooth is that you can really up the iteration level without slowing down your viewport. In the past, keeping the iteration level at 3 or 4 would really hit your video card pretty hard. But with the new TurboSmooth, you can work very quickly, even at high iteration levels.

After applying TurboSmooth, you go back down your stack and highlight the Editable Poly.

Figure 9-4: Highlight the Editable Poly.

Notice that when you highlight Editable
Poly, your box pops back to its original
shape before the TurboSmooth. That's
because you are viewing that part of the
stack. Now if you want to view the top
result of your stack, even while working
at the bottom of the stack, you press
the Show End Result button.

This will allow you to work in Edit
Poly mode while viewing your Edit Poly
object smoothed! This is glorious! To
see just how this works, make sure you
are at the bottom of your stack and

*Figure 9-5: Choose the
Show End Result button
to view the top result of
the stack.*

select Vertex mode. You'll notice an orange outline representing the bottom of your stack, even though you are viewing the
top of it.

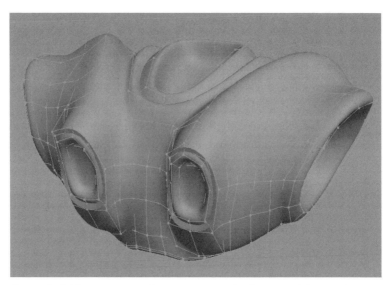

Figure 9-6: The orange outline represents the bottom of the stack.

Notice that the orange cage and the gray shaded cage move together.

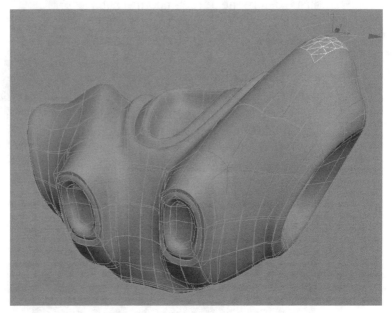

Figure 9-7: The orange cage represents the low-rez mesh and the gray shaded version shows the high-rez version.

You also have the option of toggling the Show End Result button if you want to work without viewing the top of your stack all the time.

Chapter 10

Organic Modeling Exercise: Creating a Basic Character

Yes, that's right — we're going to create the world's most basic character. This chapter's sole purpose is to show you the absolute basics for blocking out a full character. Some people prefer to build in pieces. If that's the case, you'll build out a head, an arm, a torso, and a leg. When you're all done, you'll piece it together one limb at a time. Others prefer to build a very basic mesh like we are going to do in this exercise. You'll "block" out your character and add detail after you get your basic shape. At the end of this chapter you should have a basic 3D stick figure.

Torso and Arms

Like with most things, we are going to start with a box. Let's work on the torso first. Begin with a box and collapse it to an editable mesh. Let's assume that the top polygon will be the shoulders of our character. With that in mind, grab the bottom polygon and pull it down to about waist level. Using the Scale tool, go ahead and broaden the shoulders and nip in the waist a bit. Your character should look like Figure 10-1.

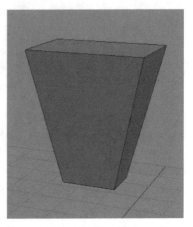

Figure 10-1: The beginning of the torso.

Almost done! Okay, not really. We are going to need to add some connections to the torso area in order to create a more realistic shape. Using the Connect tool, grab all the vertical edges (the "edge ring") and connect them with three segments.

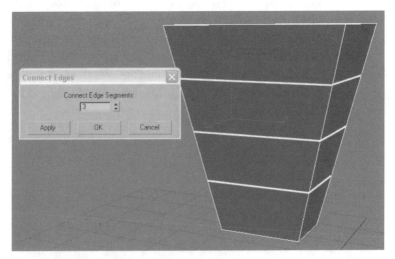

Figure 10-2: Connect the vertical edges.

Now that we have a few more edge loops to work with, let's start to tweak our character's front and side profile a bit.

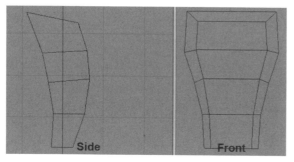

Figure 10-3: Pull and push a few edges to refine the shape.

Don't forget to use the handy selection tricks that we talked about earlier in the book. Use your Edge Ring and Edge Loop selection buttons. Select one horizontal edge on our character's chest and select Edge Ring, then connect those edge rings with three segments.

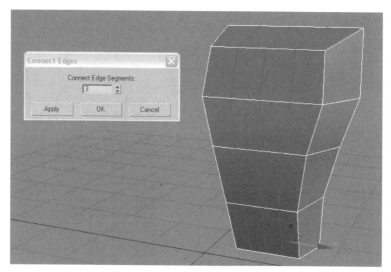

Figure 10-4: Connect the edge segments of the horizontal edge.

After adding your new cuts, spend a few minutes positioning your new detail. Your model should start looking like more of an organic shape at this point. It will become less and less "boxy" as we continue.

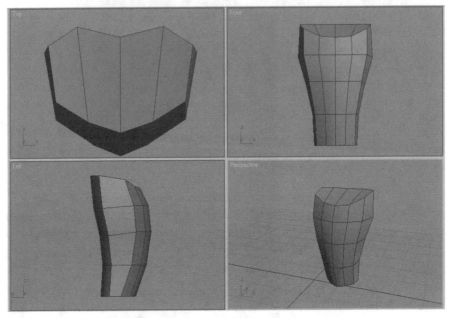

Figure 10-5: Tweak the torso a bit more.

This is really our basic torso shape at this point. From here on out, it's just about adding detail. I'm going to add a couple more edge loops to add some specific detail. I'll run one up the side of our character and one underneath his chest area to define his rib cage.

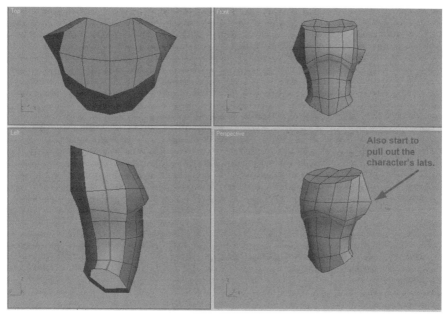

Figure 10-6: Add a few more edge loops and adjust the lats.

If you have not done so yet, now would be a good time to use the Symmetry modifier. In your Front view, delete the entire left half of your model. Now you can apply the Symmetry modifier. Make sure your Mirror axis is set to the Y axis. If Y does not work, that means you set something up differently than I did. You may need to check the Flip check box in your Symmetry options. The Symmetry modifier will mirror everything you are doing on one side, and apply those changes to the opposite side in real time.

With the torso complete, we are going to grab the polygons on the side that will define his arm. We just need to grab those polygons and extrude them off to the side. Since we have the Symmetry modifier applied, it should be doing this on the other side at the same time.

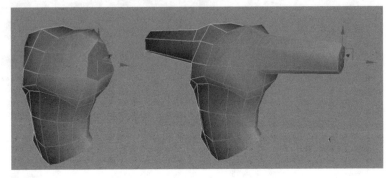

Figure 10-7: Extrude the polygons to create the arm.

Let's repeat that process one more time and extrude out the forearms. After pulling out the forearm, I'll make a couple of quick cuts so I can adjust the profile a bit and we should be good to go! The model should look something like this:

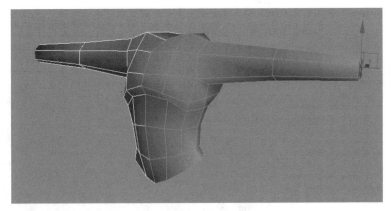

Figure 10-8: The upper arms and forearms are extruded.

Next let's make some connections. You don't need to do exactly what I'm doing at this point; in fact, you don't really need to add any at all if you don't want to. I am adding some cuts in order to create a little bit more detail for the arms and chest.

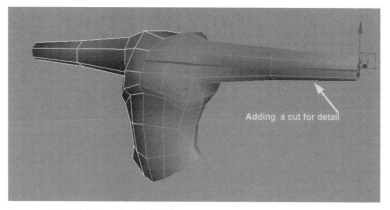

Figure 10-9: Adding detail for the arms.

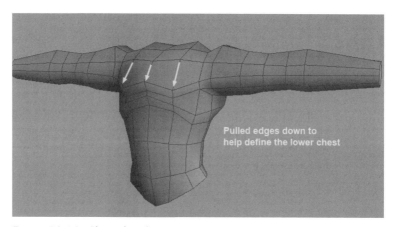

Figure 10-10: Chest detail.

Just for fun I decided to apply TurboSmooth to see how it's starting to look with greater detail.

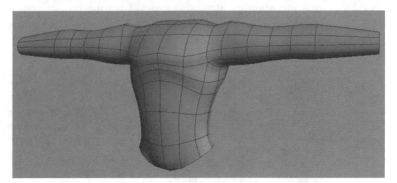

Figure 10-11: TurboSmooth to add detail.

Well, that's about it for the torso. To be honest, we didn't even need to get this detailed. This is looking pretty good now, so let's go ahead and move on to the legs.

Legs

The legs are pretty simple when you think about it. Really they are just two tubes, right? For the most part, our shape is created for us. We just need to grab the polys that will become our legs and extrude. Grab the appropriate faces, as shown in Figure 10-12.

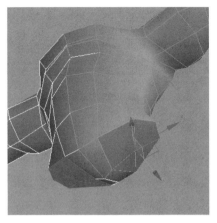

Figure 10-12: These faces are
extruded to form the leg.

After selecting the appropriate edges, extrude them and pull
them down all the way to where the ankles would be.

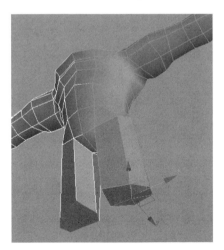

Figure 10-13: Extrude the legs.

After pulling the legs down we need to define his buttocks and
undercarriage a bit. To do that we need to add some edge
loops. Pay close attention to our character's side profile. Make
sure you give his back some arch and his buttocks some

cushion! I'm going to add an edge loop around these high-lighted edges. This will help add more curve to his backside.

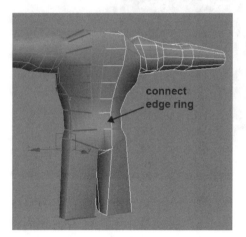

Figure 10-14: Add an edge loop.

After adding your edge loop, pull the points out to smooth out your character. Be sure to look at your character's side profile often. After making the adjustments to your new edge loop, your character's profile should look something like this:

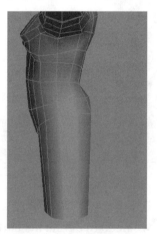

Figure 10-15: The side profile.

We obviously need to adjust the side profile a bit more. Let's add one more edge loop high on his thigh and make our adjustments.

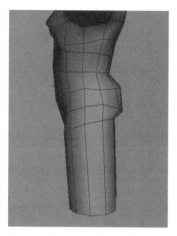

Figure 10-16: Add another edge loop.

Now what we want to do is select the open edge at the bottom of his thigh. (Use the Border sub-object selection to do this quickly.) After selecting the open edges, do a Shift-drag downward. Bring it all the way down to the ankle and then scale it down a bit.

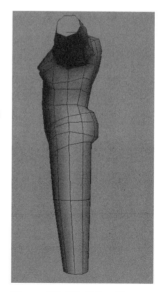

Figure 10-17: Bring the open edge down to the ankle.

This is the home stretch! Just start making horizontal connections around the leg to give it a more appropriate side profile.

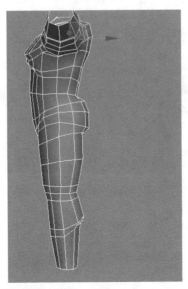

Figure 10-18: Improve the profile of the legs.

You don't have to make your leg look exactly like mine; in fact, your whole character may look different. You may want him fatter, skinnier, more stylized, etc. So don't worry if your character looks different. The only point of this is to get you started with the character creation process.

Feet

Now let's just quickly block out the foot. The way I like to do this is by grabbing the open border around the ankle and Shift-dragging it down just a bit. After pulling and creating the new polys, highlight the front four polygons and extrude them outward. Make the necessary adjustments to make it look more like a foot. Scale it down a bit and round it out.

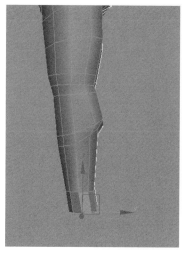

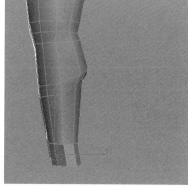

Figure 10-19: Shift-drag the ankle border downward.

Figure 10-20: Highlight the front four polys.

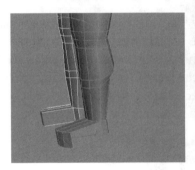

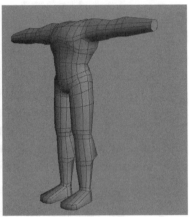

Figure 10-21: Extrude the front polys out.

Figure 10-22: Scale and adjust to make it look like a foot.

We are about done with this bad boy. Let's create a head and attach it to the torso and call him done!

Head

Here's a quick note on making the head (actually in this case, a round blob). A lot of people want to start off with either a box or a sphere. I don't like to do either. Starting with a box doesn't really make a lot of sense because we all know that the human head is round, so you may as well start off with something relatively round. On the other hand, you don't want to start with a sphere, because the geometry on a sphere is really bad. The top and bottom of a sphere come to a point, which causes a lot of unwanted triangulation.

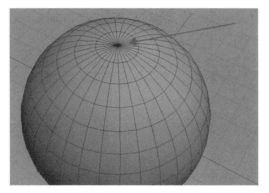

Figure 10-23: A sphere has too many triangles at the top and bottom.

A standard primitive sphere is good for being a sphere and that's about it. So, to get around this, I want you to create a cube and then apply a TurboSmooth to it. This will give you a circle but without any triangulation.

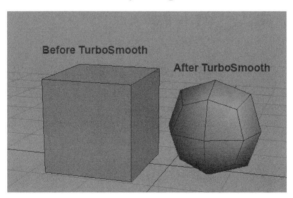

Figure 10-24: Apply TurboSmooth to a cube to get a head shape.

After you TurboSmooth the box, go ahead and collapse all the layers. Position the new "head" over the shoulders.

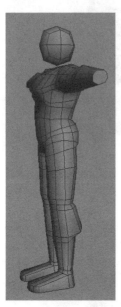

Figure 10-25: Place the head above the shoulders.

Take a few moments and just create a generic head shape. This may require a couple of cuts.

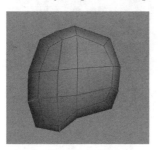

Figure 10-26: Add a few edges to make the shape look more like a head.

Done! Pretty simple, huh? Had we started with a box or used another technique, this wouldn't have gone nearly as fast. (Pats self on back.) Okay, now let's attach this head to the torso using the Bridge tool. This will be a very quick four-step process.

1. Attach the head to the body.
2. Select appropriate polygons.
3. Select the open borders.
4. Using the Bridge tool, connect the head to the torso.

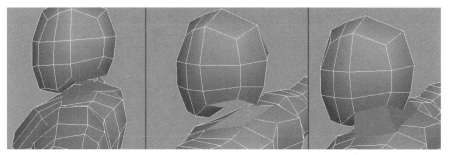

Figure 10-27: Use the Bridge tool to connect the head.

Obviously, the neck will be a bit square after we do this. So take a second or two to push and pull the verts creating the neck. Try to round it out and even move the head if necessary. When you are done, his neck should look something like this:

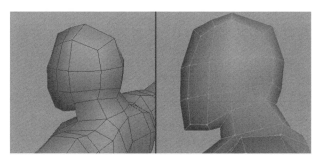

Figure 10-28: Improve the neck.

Guess what? We are done! If you got this far, you can make any other additional tweaks on your own.

What did we accomplish? We blocked out a very basic character, and we did it without using a single triangle. Our entire character is quads. In fact, if you use ZBrush or will eventually be trying out a program like that, this is the perfect starting point.

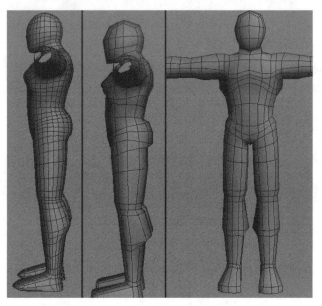

Figure 10-29: The completed character.

Chapter 11

Organic Modeling Exercise: Creating a Simple Head

Alright, kids, let's pick it up a notch! Now that we've gotten most of the basics of using the software out of the way, we can proceed to create a cool-looking character. So many books out there teach the software, but don't inspire the reader with interesting artwork. I want to try to remedy that in the remainder of this book with some interesting characters and models.

For this exercise we're going to create a simple head. We're going to do something a little more creative than making a boring old head, though. We're going to create this guy:

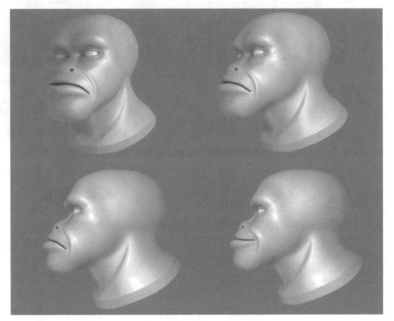

Figure 11-1: This is the character we'll end up with.

I know he looks a little complicated, but there really isn't much to this. Also note that when I walk you through the tutorial, it is not necessary to take the character to the final page. If you get 60 percent through the tutorial and you have a nice, blocked-out head and you feel you cannot continue, then stop. If that is the case, then when you are finished your character may look something like this instead:

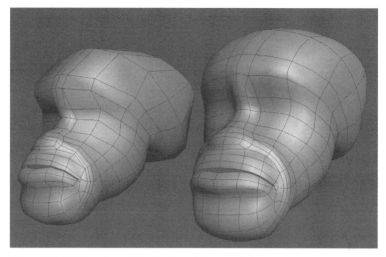

Figure 11-2: The character at the midway point.

This is totally acceptable and is a great beginning to head modeling!

Getting Proper Reference

Having something to help guide you during the process of creation is pretty important (although it's not absolutely necessary). I am one of those weird cats who will just start making things and create it as I go. I think of it as sculpting a piece of clay, I suppose. I'll add features, then take some away, and just keep making tweaks as I go until I get something interesting. This does not work from a production standpoint all the time, however. In production you usually know exactly what you want when you start. If this is the case, you most likely have a drawing or photo as a reference. For this character let's just use my final render as our reference. After you get some good reference material, it is important to set it up in a way that it will improve your workflow the most. You can place a drawing next to your monitor and kind of "eyeball" it, or you can actually create a plane in your Perspective viewport and apply the image of your reference to it. This is the approach we are going to take. You can either scan in an image of your choosing or load Side Profile.jpg from the companion files. So let's first start off by creating a plane in our Left viewport and applying the side view of our character's head onto it. When you are done, it should look something like this:

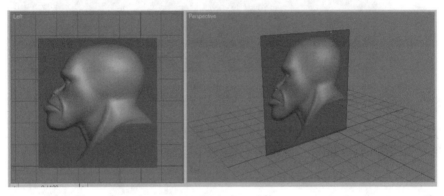

Figure 11-3: The reference image in the Left and Perspective viewports.

If you want, you can even load up a Front view in your Perspective viewport. Most of this guy's "character" comes from his side profile, however, so I think that's all we will need.

Where to Begin

Now that everything is set up, we can get started modeling! To make it easy, let's just start with a simple box. I want you to box out the entire character in the side view. What you are looking to do is to just create the character's basic head shape. Also, I'm not going to be able to go step by step for every single cut and tweak. If I did that, the book would be 3,000 pages long. I have a *job*, for God's sake! So I plan on showing you just the major steps. I will leave it up to you to use what we have learned so far to read between the lines.

Starting from the side view, let's take our box and begin creating the side profile.

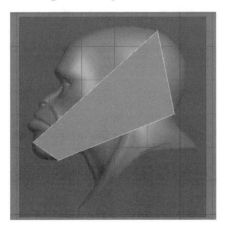

Figure 11-4: Start with the side profile and a box to create the head shape.

This is our most basic step. All I've done here is move the four verts to what I would consider to be the character's four corners.

We can't do much more now until we add more polys, so I'm going to connect the middle edges three times using the Connect tool. Then I'll move the new points around.

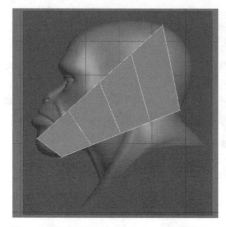

Figure 11-5: Use the Connect tool to add three segments.

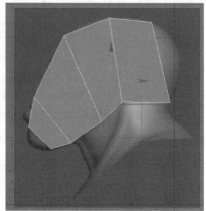

Figure 11-6: Move the points to the outer edges of the head.

 Note:

You may notice that as you create your character you think to yourself, "I can't see the reference picture anymore." This is totally normal. All you need to do is bring the Opacity setting down in your Material Editor. This will allow you to see through your mesh in order to see the reference.

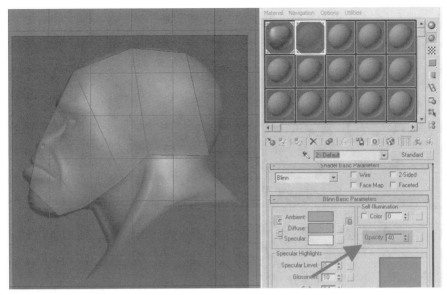

Figure 11-7: Decrease the Opacity setting of the material so you can see the underlying reference.

This is actually a pretty good start. Now that we've added a few vertical lines, let's add some horizontal lines.

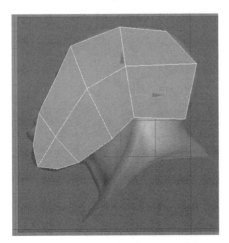

Figure 11-8: Add a few horizontal lines.

If you take a look at your character right now in Perspective view, he should look completely square on the side. We need to pull in the edges a bit just to round him out slightly.

Figure 11-9: The sides are completely square.

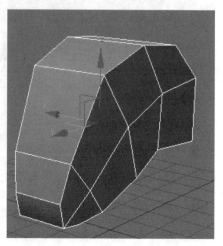

Figure 11-10: Pull the side edges out to round the head.

Now it's time to use our Symmetry modifier. Cut the head in half and delete half the head. Use the Symmetry modifier to mirror the remaining side.

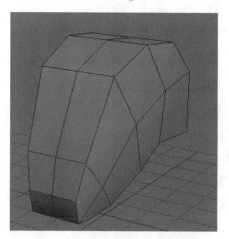

Figure 11-11: Cut the head in half and then use Symmetry to mirror it.

Now that I have the Symmetry modifier applied, I can really start moving. I'm going to do most of my modeling from the side view. Let's fast forward a bit. Continuing with the same process, I'm going to add cuts and keep blocking out my character. I'm also going to pay close attention to the Perspective view. Even though I'm doing a lot of major moves in my side view, you need to be sure to bounce back and forth from the Front and Perspective viewports to be sure that everything is arranged properly. Don't be afraid to spend time in the Perspective view moving things around and just eyeballing your model. It's okay to stray from the reference photo a bit if you want or feel the need to do so. After another couple minutes of tweaks we should have something pretty darn close to what the final model will look like.

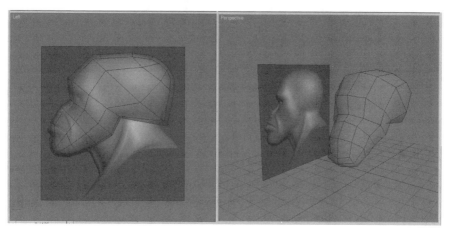

Figure 11-12: After adding cuts and tweaking, the character should look like this.

 Note:

As a rule I don't ever include the nose when I'm blocking out a character's profile. If you do that, you may quickly find that you've dug yourself into a hole with your polygon layout. Instead, I like to block out the character and then add the nose after the character is blocked.

Let's add the nose next. I usually go about creating the nose the same way on every character. Since you always have a center line for your character, simply add one more cut next to the center line.

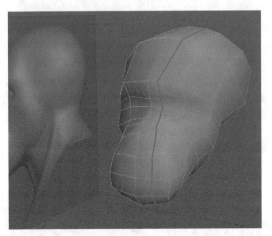

Figure 11-13: Add a cut next to the center line.

The mesh may look a little bit different, as I am making minor tweaks as I go along here. The nose setup remains the same, however. I added a cut next to the center line of the character. This center line will not only help us add lip detail, but it will provide the border of the character's nose.

Grab the faces that will make up the character's nose and do a simple bevel.

 Note:

If you are using the Symmetry modifier it's easier to collapse your mesh, then apply your bevel. You can always reapply the Symmetry modifier. If you apply an extrude or a bevel along the center line while you have the Symmetry modifier applied, you will have to go in and delete unwanted faces that it will create.

After you have completed your bevel, it should look like this:

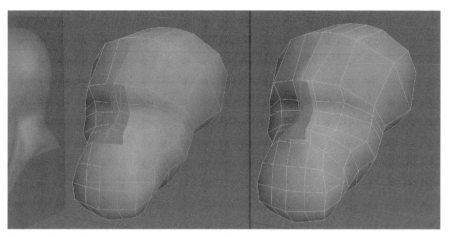

Figure 11-14: The nose faces after being beveled.

The next part is not always necessary. In fact, I don't often try to create triangles; however, for this guy I did. I target welded the top edges of the nose back to the head. If you take a look at our side profile now, you'll see we are getting pretty close.

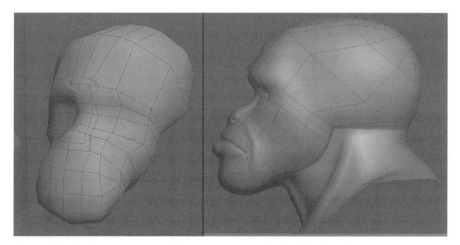

Figure 11-15: The top edges of the nose are welded to the head.

With the nose pretty well blocked out, we need to start developing the mouth. It is always very important to create the mouth properly. You need to make sure you have proper edge loops. Let's start out by grabbing the edge loop that currently traces the mouth area. When you have it selected, you need to perform a chamfer on those edges. This will create the open area of the mouth that we will be deleting shortly.

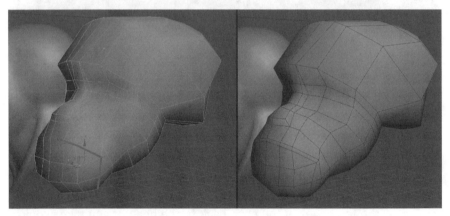

Figure 11-16: Chamfer the edge loop of the mouth.

Aha!!!! Now we are getting somewhere! The chamfer we just did will allow us to delete what will become the opening of the mouth. It will also become the edges of the lips. Use the extra polys to also help you form the character's chin. Select the polys I have highlighted in the left image of Figure 11-17 and delete them. When you are done, he should look something like the image on the right of Figure 11-17.

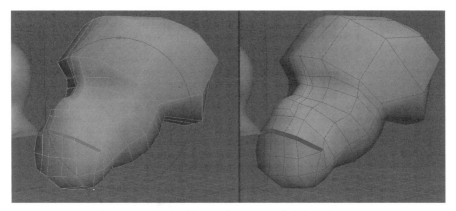

Figure 11-17: Select the polys highlighted at left and delete them.

Now that we have defined the actual mouth opening, we can pull out the lips a bit. We don't need Mick Jagger lips or anything, just more than what we have. Our first cut will be to connect the edge ring that surrounds the mouth opening.

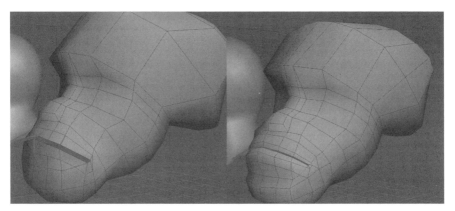

Figure 11-18: Pull out the lips by making a few new cuts.

After you make your cut, start pulling the lips out to make them seem more full. So after a few very quick tweaks and only two cuts around the mouth area, our character's profile really begins to come to life!

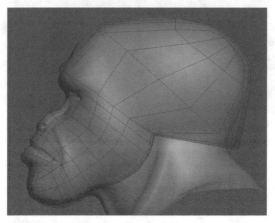

Figure 11-19: The improved lips.

Let's just make a couple more tweaks to the mouth for good measure and then we'll be about done with that part of the model. Grab the edge loop that we just created again and chamfer it one more time. This will give you one more edge loop to help really shape the profile of the lips. The last cut I want to make will be just above the chin. We'll pull this one inward a bit. This will make the chin look "stronger" and make the bottom lip look thicker. After you are done creating those two new cuts, just pull the bottom lip down a bit to create a subtle opening in the mouth.

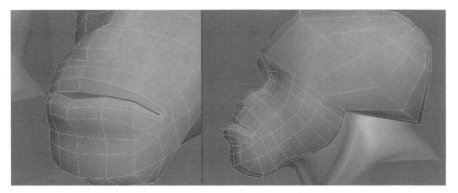

Figure 11-20: Add two new cuts to improve the lips and the chin.

Okey-dokey, I think we're done with the mouth. Let's pay attention to the nose for a bit. I'll be the first to tell you that the nose can be kinda complicated. Just don't overthink it. For the most part, a nose is a box with two holes in it. Poof! You're done! When you're starting to model a nose, just stick with the "less is more" philosophy. A lot of artists dive in and start moving around too many polygons. Keep it simple and add detail later.

Something to keep in mind when you are making a nose is your character's laugh lines.

Figure 11-21: Pay attention to the laugh lines when creating the nose.

It sounds silly, I know, but the laugh lines connect at the top of the nostrils, so it's something to be thinking about when you are creating your edge loops for the nose.

Figure 11-22: For this character, we've added edge loops for the laugh lines.

You'll see what I mean in just a bit. I'm just going to show you the basic steps I went through to create our character's nose. Feel free to ad lib a bit if you want.

I first started off by deciding exactly where his nostrils would lie on his face. I think the top corner vert of his nose will probably be just fine. Let's select it and do a simple chamfer. This will give you a very pointy nostril, but that's okay for right now because we are going to add more verts to round it out in the next couple of steps.

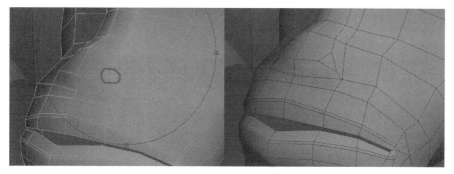

Figure 11-23: Chamfer the top corner of the nose.

Obviously, we can't let our guy breathe out of a nostril shaped like a triangle, so let's use the Cut tool now to create a cut around the edge of the nose. After your cut is made, go ahead and delete where the nostrils will be. You can cap things easily in Max, so we'll leave the hole for now. It helps me visualize what I'm doing for some reason.

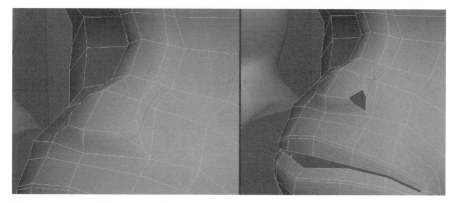

Figure 11-24: Add a cut around the edge of the nose and then delete the nostril.

This next cut is going to start the edge loop that will make up the laugh lines I was talking about earlier. Just as I said before, I'm making a cut that will go from behind the nostrils to down behind the mouth. This will make the polygons fold like actual skin when he is posed or animated. The first cut will dictate your path. After that, you need to use the Chamfer tool or Cut tool to repeat that process. You will ultimately want a few edge loops going around the nose and chin area.

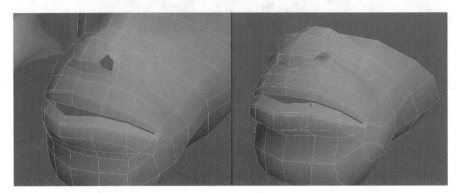

Figure 11-25: Add edge loops for the laugh lines.

I have also skipped ahead just a bit on the nostrils. I have rounded them out a bit and capped the inside using the Cap tool.

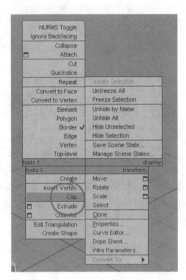

Figure 11-26: Use the Cap tool on the nostrils.

I actually created a triangle near the corner of this guy's nose. I would normally go back and clean that one triangle up. I like to have as few triangles on a model as possible. I am kind of cruising through this now, so I'm going to move forward and fix the triangle later.

The next and really the last thing we need to add on this guy is his eyes. Eyes are not that tough to do. At first they seem a bit intimidating, but there is not that much to it. Like with most things, we need to add cuts to the eye area in order to create the basic eye shape. The eye is an almond shape, so we'll need much more than the single cut we have going through the eye area now. Let's add three vertical cuts to start with.

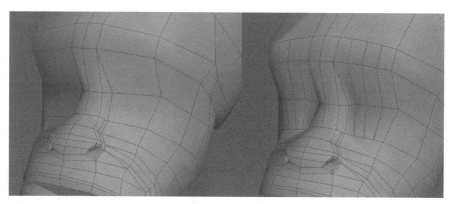

Figure 11-27: Add three vertical cuts for the eye.

 Note:

You may notice that I'm not finishing my cuts yet. They just stop at the top of the brow line. I'm just making cuts where I know I am going to need them. That's totally acceptable for right now. I will go back to the model and attach those cuts and make proper edge loops after I have my eyes looking the way I want them.

Alrighty. Now that we have our vertical cuts complete, let's do a chamfer. This will give us the basic cuts we need to start creating our eye.

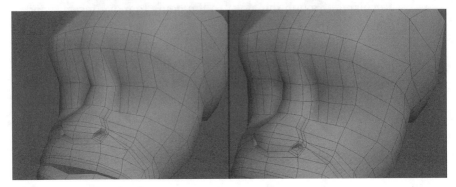

Figure 11-28: Chamfer the eye.

Now that we have the ammo we need to shape our eye, let's begin the shaping process. Go into Vertex mode and begin the basic shape of an eye. You want an almond shape. But please, for the love of God, don't make the shape symmetrical! Eyes are *not* symmetrical. If you do that I will get on a plane, fly to your house, and slap you. So let's start off on the right foot and not do that, okay?

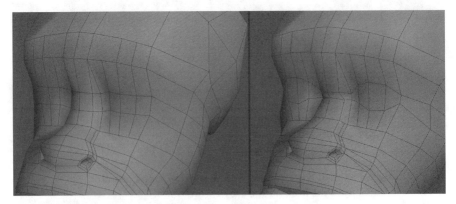

Figure 11-29: Create the eye shape.

The next few steps are very easy. Go into Polygon mode, select the eye shape, and do a bevel. You will actually do the process twice. That will help you form the eyelid area as well as create more detail around the eye.

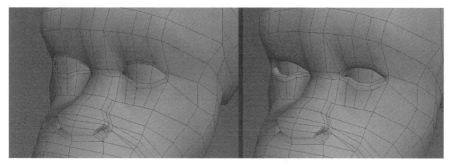

Figure 11-30: Bevel the eye shape twice to begin to create the eyelid and add detail.

With the basic eye shape complete, we need to flesh out the eyelids a bit. As you can see, right now he doesn't really have any. To do this, we are just going to add one edge loop above the top part of our eye.

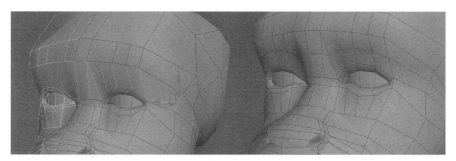

Figure 11-31: Make another edge loop for the eyelid.

We need to do a couple of things to form our character's eyelid. We need to pull the highlighted verts down toward his eye and then away. Then the verts directly below it need to come upward just a bit.

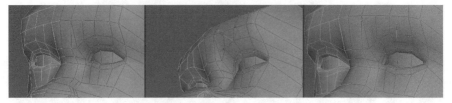

Figure 11-32: Tweak the eyelid vertices.

I'm going to start moving forward in small leaps now. I've been pretty kind so far, describing almost every move for you. I assume that if you got this far, you understand the basic modeling concepts. The point where you are right now is a perfectly acceptable stopping point; however, if you want to add more detail, you'll continue to move forward.

All I'm doing from this point on is adding detail and fixing some of those open edge loops I created earlier. Figure 11-33 shows exactly what I did. I finished off all my edge loops using the Connect tool. I also added another edge loop around the eye for detail. I decided to make the eyes a bit bigger, and pulled the brow line out even farther.

Figure 11-33: Adding further detail to the character.

Note:

It's a good idea to create the eyes and insert them into the eye sockets at this point. It will give you a guide when you begin to shape your character's eye area.

We still need to close up those open edge loops on top of our character's brow line, so we are going to make a couple of connections to finally clean that up. I also want to add more brow detail. We'll add one horizontal cut on his brow line to do that. And finally we will add one edge loop to our character's skull to round out his side profile.

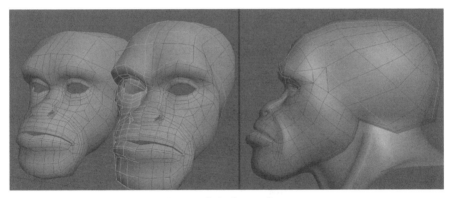

Figure 11-34: Improved brow line and skull rounding.

You'll notice that I also brought in our character's skull similar to an ape's. Figure 11-35 is a closer shot of what I ended up with.

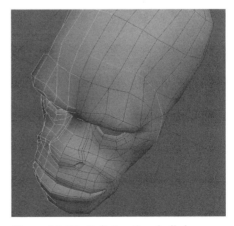

Figure 11-35: Refining the skull shape.

Our character is almost complete now. At this point I usually go in and start using Soft Selection to add character emotion. In this case I don't really have a lot to add; however, it's a great habit to get the topology of your character how you want it and then move major parts of the character using Soft Selection — especially around the eye area.

 Note:

Using Soft Selection around the eyes is a great technique. Rather than modeling your character's eyelids folded in like they would be if your eyes were open, it's much easier to just model your character with open eyes that are kind of "surprised" and then use Soft Selection to pull the brow down. This will fold the eyelids how you want without you having to model it that way.

I'm going to make some minor tweaks using Soft Selection and then apply a TurboSmooth to the character to give the final result.

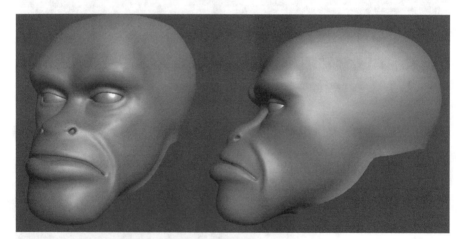

Figure 11-36: TurboSmooth for the final result.

Go now. Impress your friends with your new character!

Chapter 12

Organic Modeling Exercise: Creating a Fish

Alright, kids, this next character is a little different. Well, it's a *lot* different. Actually it's a fish. A lot of people get so wrapped up in making character heads or focusing on hard edge modeling for environment work that they don't ever think about how they'd go about making "different" characters. For this modeling exercise we are going to make a fish. I want this fish to have a very expressive personality, however, so she's going to need more of a human face attached to a fish body. Think something along the lines of *Finding Nemo*. This character is a bit different from our last one, so we don't want to start it off the same way. For this character we'll be starting off with a different part of the body. This is exactly the reason why it's good to model different kinds of characters from time to time. It teaches you to think ahead and explore other techniques that will better suit different types of characters.

Here is a preview of the character we are going to create:

Figure 12-1: The completed fish character.

As I said in the previous chapter, you don't need to take this character all the way to the finished character you see in Figure 12-1. If you start to feel overwhelmed or not confident in your abilities to continue, then you can stop at any point. You can always continue later when you feel that your abilities have progressed. So don't worry about the end result so much; we are teaching techniques here. Your abilities will progress naturally the more you practice.

Let's begin! First of all, the focus of this character seems to be on the mouth. It will be the primary focus of any potential animation. It will also be driving our character's expressions, so the mouth is very critical. With this in mind, let's start by creating the character's mouth.

The Mouth

We are going to use a slightly different technique called "edge modeling" to create the mouth. I'm going to create a surface and then extrude edges off that surface by holding the Shift key and dragging. I want you to make a plane in your Front viewport. You will find the plane in your standard primitive directory. Create a plane with eight vertical cuts.

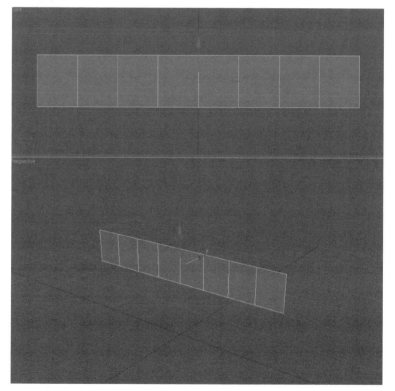

Figure 12-2: First create a plane with eight cuts.

After you create the plane, delete half of it. Collapse your plane to an Editable Polygon and delete the entire left half. Then apply the Symmetry modifier to it along the X axis.

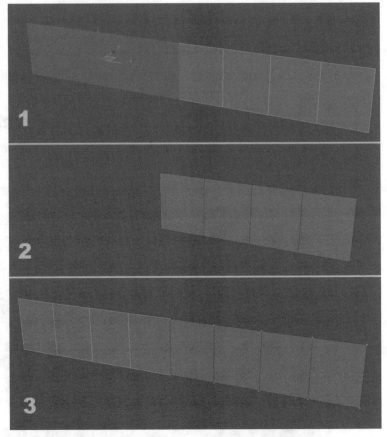

Figure 12-3: Delete the left half of the plane and then apply Symmetry along the X axis.

This is the beginning of our fish from the front! I know she doesn't look like much right now, but pretty soon we'll have the mouth created and you'll be able to see where I'm going with this.

Now that we have the building block set up to create the shape of our character's upper lip, we need to create a basic shape. Go into Vertex mode and begin to move the verts into the shape of our character's upper lip. I recommend doing this from the Front viewport.

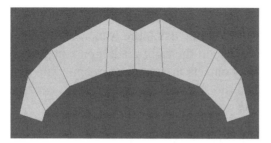

Figure 12-4: From the Front viewport, move the
verts into an upper lip shape.

This looks to be a pretty good start. Let's delete the Symmetry modifier from the top of our layer stack now. I want to mirror the upper lip down on the Y axis.

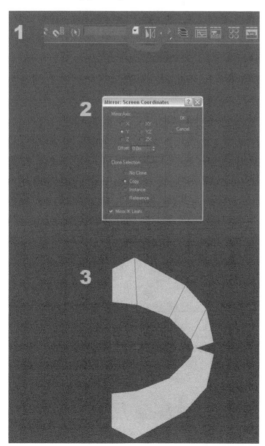

Figure 12-5:
Mirror the
upper lip on the
Y axis.

This gives us a quick starting point for both lips. Attach the bottom lip to the top lip using the Attach button in your modifier stack (it's also in the right-click menu, upper-left quad). After both poly objects are attached, reapply the Symmetry modifier along the X axis. This will give you very basic upper and lower lips.

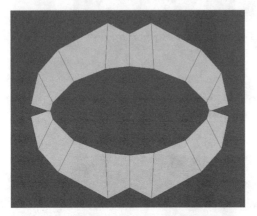

Figure 12-6: Basic upper and lower lips.

With the building blocks set I can really start moving now. Let's weld our corners up and then begin. I am going to use the Connect tool and the Move tool only for the next few minutes. I want to create a more realistic mouth shape first.

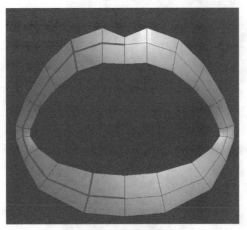

Figure 12-7: Use Connect and Move to adjust the lip shapes.

Figure 12-7 shows you the cuts that I added. I really didn't do that much, but you can see how quickly this will begin to take shape. Before we move on, I want to start to pull the corners of our character's mouth away from the front of the lips. A lot of beginners tend to end up with characters with a very flat mouth. Your mouth isn't sitting flush on your face — the corners of your mouth go back. Your character's expression will dictate how far back the corners should go. I want to use the Soft Selection feature to pull the corners back. If we begin this process now, it'll be easier than if we wait until we are dealing with more polygons later. Check the Soft Selection check box in your modifier stack and pull the corners of the mouth back. You may have to adjust your Soft Selection settings to get the right falloff.

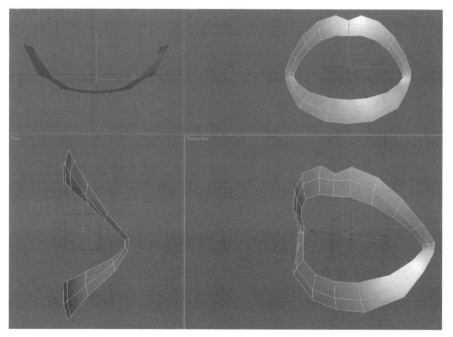

Figure 12-8: Use Soft Selection to pull the corners of the mouth back.

It's time to begin our edge modeling process. Select the entire outer edge loop on the inside of the character's mouth.

✎ **Note:**

You should be using the Select Edge Loop function in your modifier panel to speed up your workflow.

After selecting the edge loop, activate your Scale tool. While holding Shift, drag downward. This will create a new set of polygons to work with. It may scale your edges outward a bit in an undesired direction. This is normal. Just keep all the edges selected and move them back toward the center on the X axis.

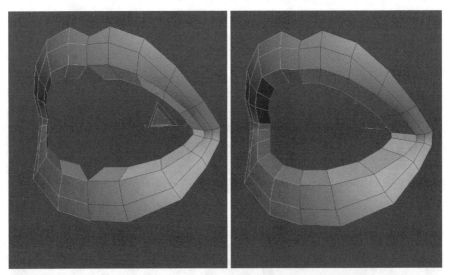

Figure 12-9: Select the edge loop and scale downward to create another set of polygons.

I am going to repeat this process one more time on the inside of the mouth and then reposition my new vertices. I'm also going to use Soft Selection to pull the corners of the mouth back one more time.

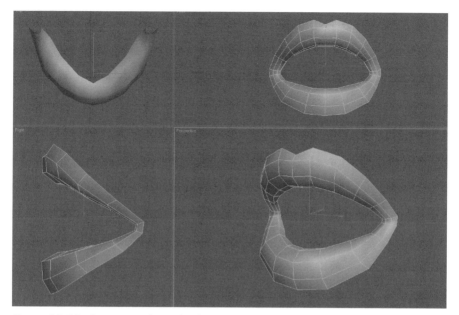

Figure 12-10: Create another edge loop, then use Soft Selection and pull the corners back.

It's definitely starting to look more like a mouth now. I just want to add a little more detail to the top and bottom lips. Lips don't just flow up into the nose; there is a very subtle ridge at the top of your lip. It's more subtle on some people than others. I want to quickly create that ridge. Select the edge loop

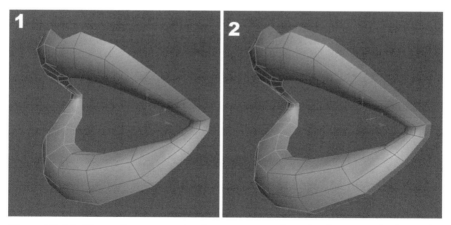

Figure 12-11: Shape the upper edge loop to create the ridge between the lip and the nose.

that makes up the entire outside of the mouth. Hold Shift and drag it back just slightly, then begin to manually position your new vertices.

I'm going to repeat this process just one more time to give myself another edge loop to work with. Now would also be a good time to apply a TurboSmooth modifier at the top of your stack to see how this will look smoothed out.

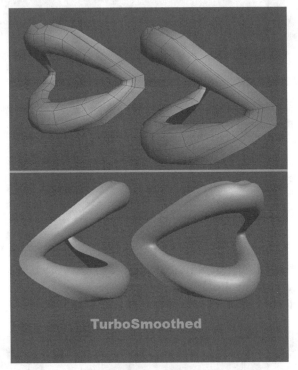

Figure 12-12: Add another edge loop, then use TurboSmooth to see how the lips look.

Now she's looking good. Okay, so I'm not going to tell you how to do every single step. The technique we have been using so far is going to carry throughout most of this character. Use the same technique to create the inside of the mouth. Grab the inner edge loop, hold Shift, and pull it back down toward the throat area. You will most likely need to do this a couple of times to make it look smooth.

The Body and Tail

It's time to turn our attention to the body.

Like you did for the lips, you want to pull out the outer edge loop to create polys that will start to create the body of our fish.

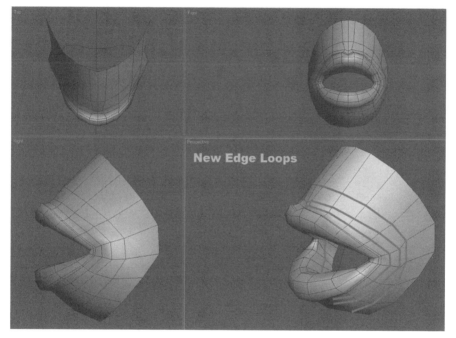

Figure 12-13: Continue to create edge loops to create the inner lips and the throat.

And again, don't forget to look at it smoothed.

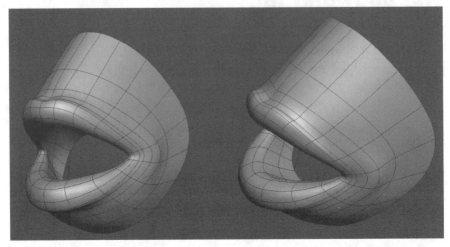

Figure 12-14: TurboSmooth the shape occasionally to see how it looks.

The next part is a big one. This will determine the overall shape of our character's body. I recommend deleting your TurboSmooth modifier and collapsing your character to make it easier when you are scaling your edge loops all the way back to the tail of your character.

In your side view, grab the edge loop that is farthest back. Hold Shift and pull it back and scale it up. You are going to repeat this process about seven times or so. Once you start, it should only take you a minute or so. Manually tweak as you go to get the proper shape.

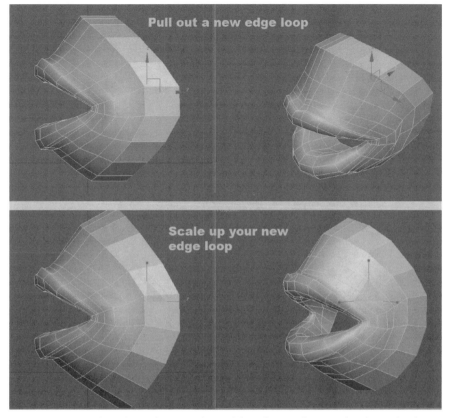

Figure 12-15: Delete the TurboSmooth modifier, then pull new edge loops back to start creating the body.

Now repeat this process multiple times to create the overall shape of your fish. Don't forget to refer to your Top and Perspective viewports to make sure that your character looks good from all sides. You don't want your fish to look good from the side but flat from the top; she should be smooth all over. So tweak the vertices accordingly.

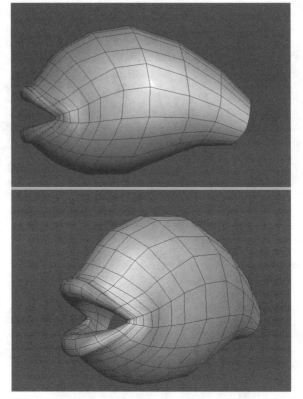

Figure 12-16: Continue to add and refine edges.

Okay, we definitely have the major portions of the fish done. That didn't take too long, did it? I'm going to skip how to make the tail because it's the same thing that we have been doing. Just keep pulling out polys and shape it how you see fit. I want to fast forward to creating a really animated expression on our character's face using Soft Selection. This will also demonstrate the importance of proper edge loops.

Delete half your fish again and reapply a Symmetry modifier to your model. If you don't have a TurboSmooth modifier at the top of your stack, make sure you have it applied also. Anytime you're creating some kind of facial expression or wrinkle, you need to know that such detail will come out right in your high-poly version. Go to the bottom of your stack and, in Face or Vertex mode, grab the corner of your fish's mouth. Check the Soft Selection check box in your Modify panel to the right. Adjust the falloff to the desired setting.

 Note:

You don't want your falloff to be too much or too little. You may move the selected verts and not like the result. Just undo one step and adjust your falloff accordingly.

Grab the corner of your fish's mouth and pull it back and up. Because you created your fish with proper edge loops, it will automatically create a very realistic expression. You'll notice that the corners of the mouth go up and into the cheek and

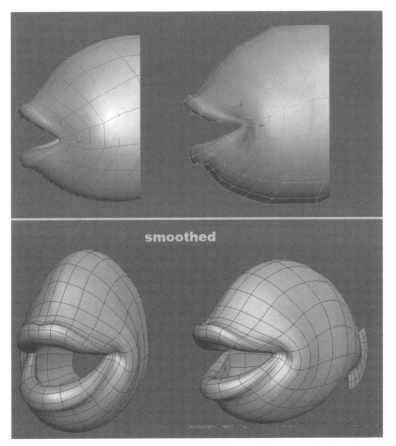

Figure 12-17: Using Soft Selection, pull the mouth corner back and up.

fold properly. When you are done, she should look something like Figure 12-17.

She's looking pretty cool! She still needs a little more detail, however, before she will start to have her own personality.

The Fins

Let's extrude out a pectoral fin on the side, then quickly add the dorsal fin to complete the profile. First, add an edge loop all the way across the top of your fish. We need to do this for two reasons: to help define the cleft above the lip and to give us one more loop to extrude the dorsal fin. Begin by selecting the proper edge ring and connecting it.

Figure 12-18: Add an edge loop across the top for the dorsal fin.

Now that we have our new set of polygons, we need to extrude the new fin straight up. The initial shape is not important. Just create the polys; you can always modify them later.

 Note:

Don't forget that if you extrude along the symmetry edge, it will create unwanted inner faces. This is normal. Just delete them.

Your initial extrusion should look something like this:

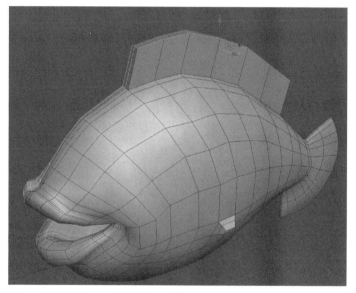

Figure 12-19: Extrude the dorsal fin up.

Continue to modify the dorsal fin on your own. You'll need to add one or two horizontal cuts to the fin in order to really make it look organic.

The Teeth

In the meantime, let's work on a set of teeth. These are going to be extremely basic and you should be able to create them in just a few quick steps. Create a box with about eight width segments. Apply an Edit Poly modifier, then scale the top faces closer together, making kind of a wedge shape. Apply a Bend modifier to the entire box; you should be bending it about 180 degrees. Apply one more TurboSmooth, and that's it for the teeth.

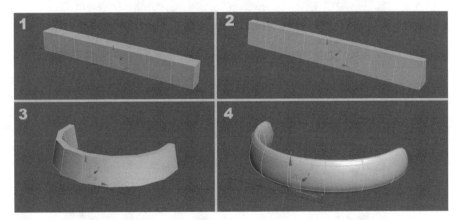

Figure 12-20: Simple teeth.

All that is left now is to place the teeth. You may want to go back into your stack to make very minor adjustments to make sure that the teeth will fit in the fish's mouth properly.

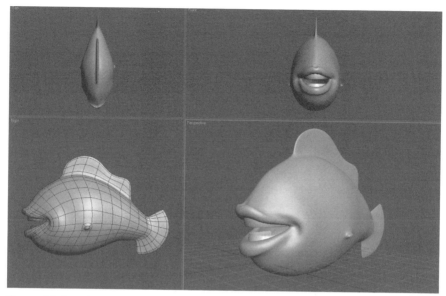

Figure 12-21: Place the teeth in the mouth.

We are almost done! The last part of this character is going to be her eyes.

The Eyes

There are several ways to go about creating eyes. Personally, I like to start off with some kind of reference. Since the skin around the eye needs to hug the eye precisely, I like to create the eyes first and then model around the eyes to ensure that it will be a perfect fit.

Create two spheres that will represent the eyes and place them on the character where you want them.

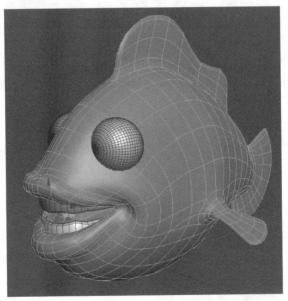

Figure 12-22: Create two spheres and place them.

This will give us a really good modeling target. Now all we need to do is create the eye opening and the brow area.

 Note:

Toggle the eye on and off frequently to make sure you are headed in the right direction.

Just like the previous character, I am going to start the eye area off by chamfering a vert. Let's hide the eye for a second and chamfer the vertex highlighted in Figure 12-23. After you apply a chamfer, go ahead and delete the new polygon that it created.

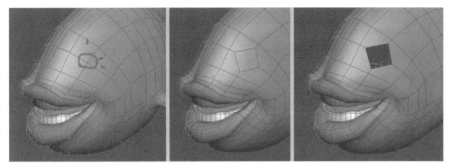

Figure 12-23: Chamfer the vertex and delete the new polygon.

This result is exactly what we want. The next step is to round out the eye opening. To do that we need to make a series of edge loops. You'll want to think about this for a second before you just go connecting edges or cutting up your mesh. The goal is to have nice clean edge loops surrounding the eye. With that in mind, let's begin making the first cuts.

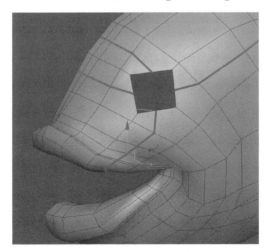

Figure 12-24: Begin making cuts for edge loops around the eye.

After you make these new cuts you need to make the necessary adjustments to round out the eye. Be sure to toggle on TurboSmooth from time to time also.

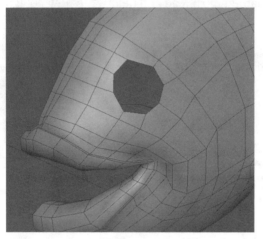

Figure 12-25: Adjust the edges to round the shape.

At least we have an eye shape at this point, which is a great start. From here, you'll want to continue pushing the eye shape outward to make the opening bigger. In the process you may notice you need to make a couple of new cuts. After you are done, you should have an eye opening that is pretty close to finished.

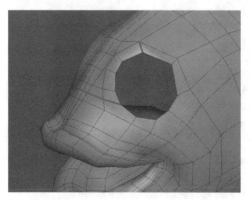

Figure 12-26: Make a few new cuts and open up the eye.

I need to add just a few more loops for good measure. Let's add another ring around the eye that connects to the lip to make the eye a little more round, and one more on the body just behind the eye.

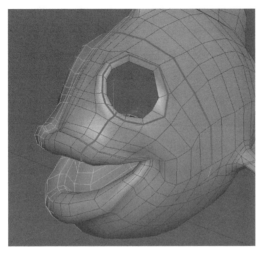

Figure 12-27: Add an edge ring to round the eye shape and another behind the eye.

Finishing Up

This is as far as I'm going to take you. If you got this far, then you will most certainly be able to make any necessary changes from here such as finishing the eyes and adding other details. I would suggest, however, to start using Soft Selection a bit at this point. Make sure you raise the eyebrows higher. Also think about pulling her cheeks out. Both of these adjustments will make the eye look really embedded in the head and skin. You may even have to add just a few more polys in various places to get the right look. My finished geometry looks like Figure 12-28.

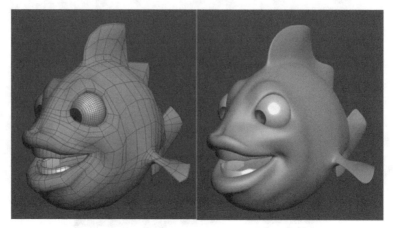

Figure 12-28: The final character.

Chapter 13

Spline Modeling

Understanding How Spline Modeling Works

We have focused a lot on poly modeling up to this point, and I will continue to focus on it in later chapters as well. Poly modeling is probably the most common form of modeling in today's major 3D packages. There are many ways to make things, however, and only being familiar with one way will limit your abilities and speed as a 3D modeler.

The way spline modeling works is that you create a "cage" and then apply a surface to that cage. Think of it like shaping chicken wire, except this is really cool chicken wire. Once you have your spline cage complete, you apply a surface to that cage. Now what is really nice is that you can go down in your layer stack and continue to modify your surface using the original splines. That means you can adjust your surface using the Bezier handles provided on the original splines. This actually gives you a lot more control than traditional polygon modeling because of the handles. It also causes fewer headaches than using good old nurbs.

Creating the Spline Cage

Let's use the Spline tool to create a spline cage in the Perspective viewport. I don't want to make anything specific right now; I just want to show you two different ways to create the cage.

Starting off in the Perspective viewport, I want you to create a generic shape on the floor. Try not to make it too complicated. Let's use only four or five vertices. The more you create, the longer it will take to create the cage, so don't go too crazy.

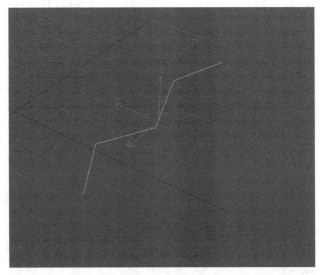

Figure 13-1: Use four or five vertices to create a shape.

The next thing I want to do is adjust the handles. By default they are probably set to be Corner. Let's just make them all Smooth instead for right now. Go into Vertex mode, highlight all the verts, and right-click. In the upper-left quad, select Smooth. Your spline will smooth out, getting rid of all your edges.

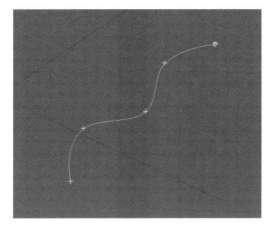

Figure 13-2: Smooth all the handles.

All we want to do now is copy this spline. Do a Shift-drag to the left and make sure you set it to Copy. You should have two identical shapes now in your Perspective viewport.

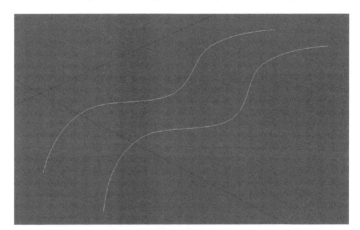

Figure 13-3: Shift-drag and copy the shape.

Now it's time to begin creating the actual cage. The goal is to connect these two splines with segments, similar to edges and polygons. Activate the Snap tool and set it to End Point. This will snap your cursor to the vertices in your spline. What we need to do is just create individual splines between these two lines. Using the Line tool, snap a new spline vert to vert (like connect-the-dots).

Figure 13-4: Begin to create splines between the vertices.

 Note:

Left-click to start your connecting spline, and left-click to snap it to its corresponding vert, then right-click to finish.

After you connect everything, it should look like this:

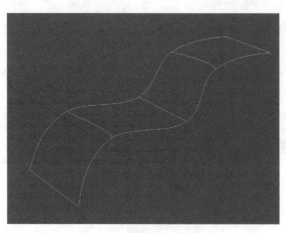

Figure 13-5: Completed spline cage.

Applying a Surface to the Spline Cage

This is our cage in all its glory! The next thing we need to do is attach all these splines so that Max views them as a single spline. Right now it is made up of seven individual spline shapes, so select any of the splines and activate the Attach button in the Modify panel, under the Edit Geometry rollout.

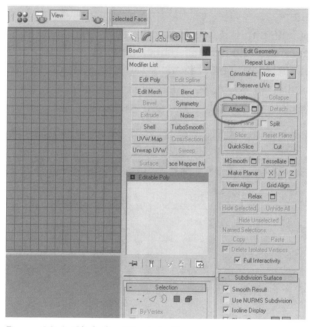

Figure 13-6: Click the Attach button.

This puts you in Attach mode. You'll notice now that if you cursor over a spline your cursor changes. That means you are over an attachable spline. Just left-click that desired spline and it becomes attached.

✎ **Note:**

You don't ever really need to weld spline verts together for your cage to be complete. You only need to have the spline vertices close to each other (very close), but they don't ever really need to be welded. Max will figure it out on its own when we create our surface.

Now that the spline is a single object, we want to apply a surface modifier to our cage. Select Surface in the Modify panel. Immediately after you do that, your cage should have a surface applied to it. If it does not, then that means you simply need to check the Flip Normals check box in the surface modifier rollout. Max doesn't really know if you want the surface to point up or down, so it may choose wrong. If it does, just check the box and you're good to go.

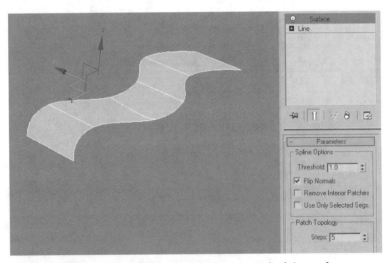

Figure 13-7: You may need to choose Flip Normals if the surface modifier does not show up.

At the bottom of the surface modifier you'll notice the Patch Topology area. The Steps setting will dictate how smooth/detailed you want your surface. Let's just make it 5.0 for right now; that's pretty smooth.

I know right now the spline cage doesn't look like much, but that's because we haven't moved anything yet. Let's go to the bottom of our layer stack and select Line again to take us to the original spline cage. Also make sure that the Show End Result button is pressed. (This allows us to see how our modifications to the cage affect the end result.)

Figure 13-8: Select Line from the Surface layer stack and press the Show End Result button.

Adjusting the Splines

Now go into Vertex mode and start moving some of the vertices around. Note that you'll have to draw a selection box around any verts you want to select. Why? Because we didn't weld those verts together. So if you just click on one, you'll leave the others behind, and that will destroy the surface. The surface is held together based on the fact that the verts are close to each other. I'm going to just move some things around and create a nifty little shape now.

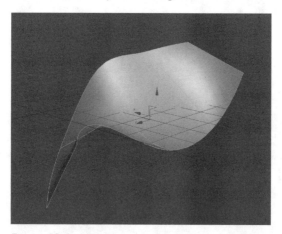

Figure 13-9: Move some vertices around to create a neat shape.

Alright now, let's say that I'm not too happy with this shape, and I need more detail in the middle in order to create another "lump" or something. You would just redo the original process onto this existing cage. In this case I want to create a cut through the center of this cage. Select vertices and right-click. In the bottom-left quad you have a Refine option.

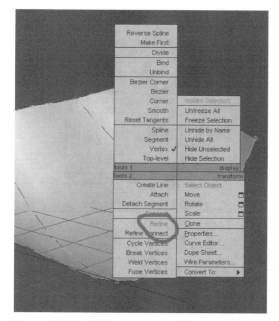

Figure 13-10: Select vertices and right-click, then select the Refine option.

Selecting Refine takes you into Refine mode. Refine will add new vertices anywhere you left-click on your spline. Let's add one to the middle of each edge we want to divide.

Note:

In this case you may want to turn off the Show End Result button so you can better see what you're doing.

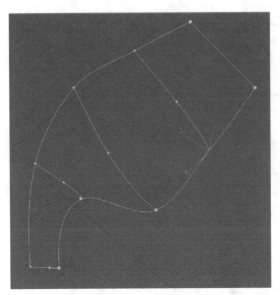

Figure 13-11: Add new vertices to the middle of each edge you want to divide.

Score! Now that we have the verts we need, let's add the edges we need. I'll show you one final trick here. Just above the Attach button in the Geometry rollout is a button called Create Line. This will create a new line but keep it part of your existing cage. This will prevent you from having to make new splines and then attach when you're done. The line is considered to be part of the object to begin with. (You could have also done that in the beginning, but I wanted to show you two ways of doing this.)

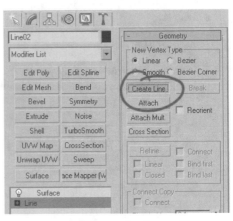

Figure 13-12: Choose the Create Line button to automatically make the new line part of the existing cage.

After selecting the Create Line button, you need to activate your snaps again. This will ensure you create a spline off the existing verts. Start at the left and just click your way to the right, making your new edges along the way. When you are done, just right-click. Your cage should now have a nice cut down the middle of it. Because these are brand-new segments, they will come in as Corner splines. That's too angular. We want them to match the other smooth ones, so select all the new vertices you created and change them to Smooth.

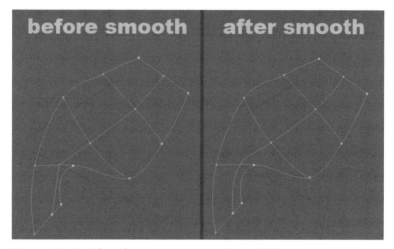

Figure 13-13: Select the new vertices and smooth them.

Done! We have a glorious new cut down the middle of our cage. Go ahead and turn back on the Show End Result button so you can see your surface. Next, I'm going to make a couple more tweaks and show you my end result.

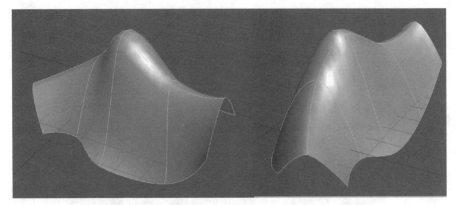

Figure 13-14: After a few more tweaks, the spline cage looks like this.

Pretty simple stuff! I would encourage you to go back into your vertices and adjust your vert settings from Smooth to Corner, Bezier, Bezier Corner, etc., and practice adjusting your splines using the handles provided. Good luck!

Chapter 14

Spline Modeling Exercise: Creating the Hull of a Boat

In the previous chapter I showed you how to use Max's spline tools to make a very basic spline surface. In this chapter we'll use those techniques to create the basic outline of a boat hull. This is actually a perfect example of when to use spline tools. You'll also use the spline tools if you are doing certain types of architectural modeling, such as making a complex roof shape. It's great to spline out the shapes you need from the top and side view and then apply your surface. Trying to do something similar using polygons is brutal. Unfortunately, most people (even good modelers) live and die using box modeling as their only technique.

If you need to use some form of reference, then by all means do so. This is a relatively easy shape, so I'm not going to use any.

The very first thing that I want to do is create the side profile of our boat.

Note:

When you make your initial shape, make something very basic.

We will go back and tweak our shape after it is blocked out a bit.

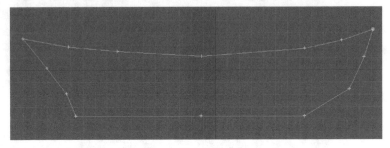

Figure 14-1: Create the side profile of the boat hull.

I know, I know, this looks like a pretty ugly boat. So we're going to have to make some changes. Adjust your vertices one vert at a time. Different vertices will need different settings. The final adjusted image should look much more detailed.

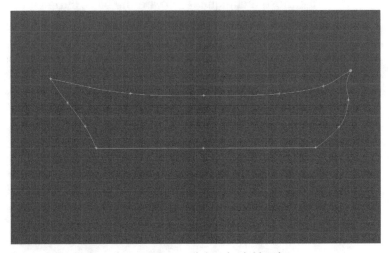

Figure 14-2: Adjust the vertices until they look like this.

So you can see what I did, I marked what I changed each vertex to in Figure 14-3.

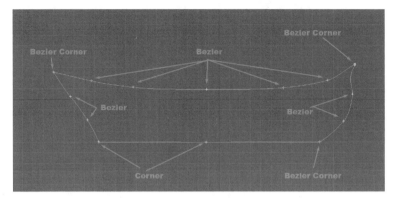

Figure 14-3: The vertex shapes.

 Note:

You can adjust the smoothness of your splines by adjusting the spline interpolation in the Interpolation rollout of your line modifier. I kept mine at 6.0. You should also know that a higher interpolation may result in a higher polygon count.

Now let's not forget that we work in three dimensions. We need to modify our boat from the top and front views as well. All we really have at this point is a flat shape from the front. Modify the current shape to be more three-dimensional. You can tell in the Perspective viewport that it's starting to look more like a boat.

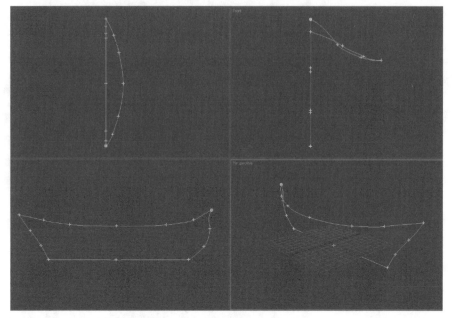

Figure 14-4: Modify the shape to be three-dimensional.

With our basic boat shape complete, I need to start making the connecting edges.

 Note:

Always make your edges as clean as possible. This means with as few triangles as you can get away with. So we may need to add vertices just in order to make this surface clean.

After looking at my initial shape and vertex layout, I decide I will definitely need to add a couple of verts in order for my mesh to be what I would consider "clean." With that in mind, I am going to use the Refine tool to add four vertices in order to clean up my edges.

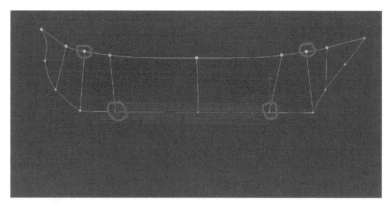

Figure 14-5: Add four vertices.

Check out that bad boy! Not a single triangle! Don't forget that you might need to tweak these new verts in order to keep your splines smooth.

We have enough to create our surface now. Let's go ahead and apply the surface modifier to see where we stand.

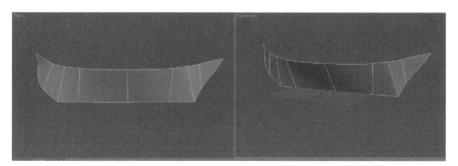

Figure 14-6: Apply a surface modifier.

As expected, it looks pretty flat. Let's add one horizontal cut across the boat. After we make the cut, we'll need to pull out those new verts to give the boat more thickness.

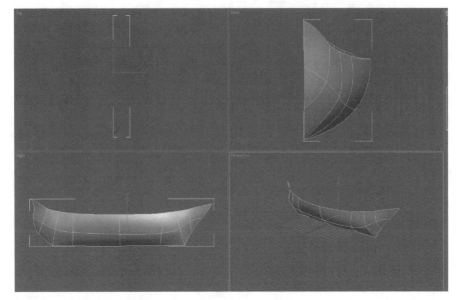

Figure 14-7: Add a horizontal cut to give the hull more thickness.

This is a perfect starting point for our basic hull. Remember that we are using the splines to create a basic shape, not to create the boat from start to finish. I still prefer to use polygons when modeling.

Since we are happy with this shape, we are ready to collapse it to polygons.

 Note:

The number of surface steps determines how many polys you will have when you collapse it. I don't recommend having any steps when you collapse your surface, so make your Steps setting 0. You can always TurboSmooth the shape if you want to add more polys.

Set Steps to 0 and collapse your new surface.

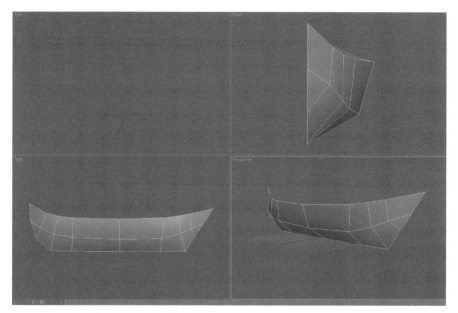

Figure 14-8: Set the number of surface steps to 0 and collapse the surface.

With our final polygon layout completed and collapsed, the next step is to apply the Symmetry modifier so we can see what the full hull will look like.

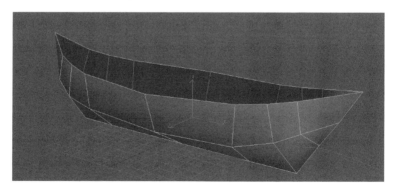

Figure 14-9: Apply Symmetry to see the full hull shape.

Obviously we can't sail away in our boat if it doesn't have any thickness to it. Right now it's paper thin and has no interior. Fortunately Max has a modifier called the Shell tool that solves this problem for you. What's the Shell modifier? you ask. The Shell modifier solidifies or gives thickness to an object by adding an extra set of faces facing the opposite direction of existing faces, plus edges connecting the inner and outer surfaces wherever faces are missing in the original object. You can specify offset distances for the inner and outer surfaces, characteristics for edges, material IDs, and mapping types for the edges. Clear as mud, huh? In short, it'll make thin stuff fat.

Apply the Shell modifier and adjust the Inner and Outer settings to your liking.

After applying the modifier you should have something like this:

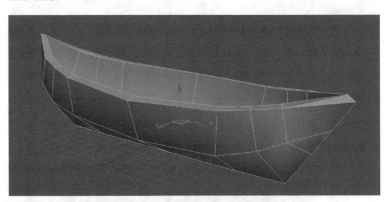

Figure 14-10: The hull after applying the Shell modifier.

Now that we have added thickness to our geometry, we need to up the poly count to smooth out our boat. Add the TurboSmooth modifier now to the top of your stack and up your iteration count to 3.0. That will give you a nice smooth result.

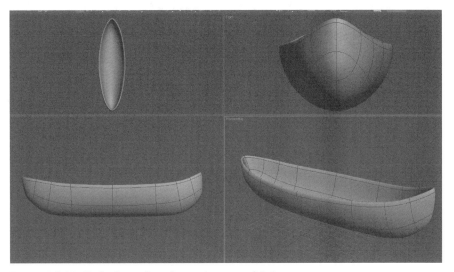

Figure 14-11: TurboSmooth with an iteration of 3.0.

Now you can add your own detail. Maybe a busty mermaid hanging off the front, or a mast and some sails. I've turned the shape into a canoe by adding a couple of seats and a support beam underneath it.

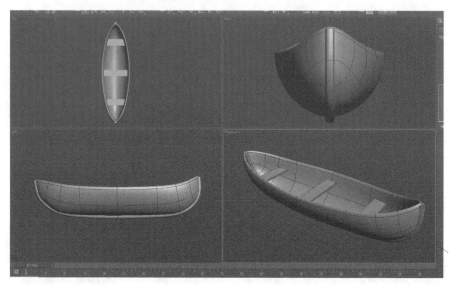

Figure 14-12: Add some detail to the hull to make it look like the type of boat you want.

All done! That's it for our spline modeling exercise! Go make your daddy proud!

Chapter 15

Becoming an Advanced Modeler/Artist

Don't Make Common Industry Mistakes

There is a pretty big difference in being a good modeler/artist and being a professional. If you think that simply being good at modeling or texturing or animating will get you far in your professional career, you would be incorrect. Now don't get me wrong. You need good art, and creating that good art will get your foot in the door and even get you jobs. So having a strong portfolio is crucial. However, if you wish to keep your job, you will need to be professional and take certain things into consideration when making your art and dealing with a team environment.

Building a proper mesh is very important. Whether you are doing organic character modeling or environmental hard surface modeling, building a proper mesh is crucial for several reasons. First and foremost, if you are going to eventually texture your geometry, having a clean mesh will make it 7,234,738,472,834 times easier to unwrap your character and paint him. Secondly, if you ever intend to animate your geometry, it must be modeled properly in order to move accordingly. A poor mesh will cause pinching, creasing, clipping, etc. Besides that, if your mesh looks like a can of Silly String that blew up on a hot summer day...well, that's just ugly.

Figures 15-1 through 15-3 show examples of correct and incorrect edge flow.

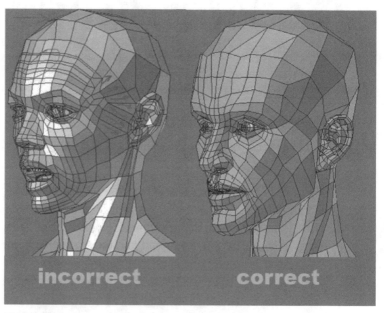

Figure 15-1

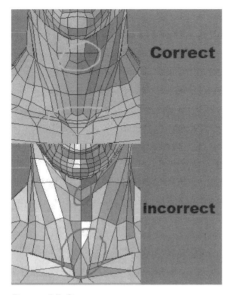

Figure 15-2

Figure 15-3

Understand How Animation Will Affect Your Geometry

If you are creating geometry that will eventually be animated, then you have to model it properly. A lot of beginners worry about creating a model that looks good in the standard "T" pose, but they don't think past their own task. You have to understand how anatomy works and where to create proper edge loops in order for your character to work properly.

This figure is how most beginners would start out.

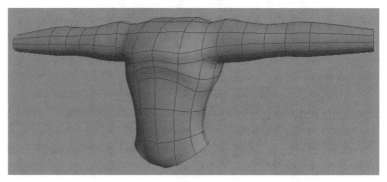

Figure 15-4: As basic as this model is, it is already starting off with incorrect edge loops.

They'd create the torso and then extrude out the arms thinking, "Well, that's what it looks like." But they have not taken into consideration the rotation of the shoulder and how that affects the chest. If you look at your chest and hold your arms out, you'll notice that a very distinct line is drawn from the bottom of your pectoral muscles, and it flows up the front of your armpit and all the way around your deltoid.

Figure 15-5: A line is created by the bottom of the pectoral muscles that extends to the deltoid.

You can see this very clearly when looking at bodybuilders. In fact, they make great references if you are unsure exactly how muscles are laid out under the skin.

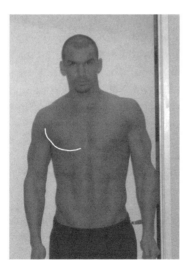

Figure 15-6   *Figure 15-7*

If you create proper edges that follow the flow from the chest to the shoulder, you will get very realistic and proper deformation in your character.

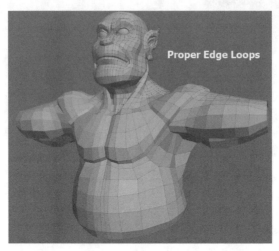

Figure 15-8: Basic model with edge loops added.

This model was built properly. You can see how the bottom of the chest flows up into the shoulder intentionally. You can also see how accurately it deforms when moved. If you tried to do the same rotations with the character in Figure 15-4, it would never deform properly and would not look at all natural.

Likewise, when dealing with the face you need to use similar rules. You can't simply create the profile of a face and assume it will deform properly. There are many things to consider. When the character smiles, will his cheeks be able to rise properly?

Figure 15-9: Notice how the checks rise when the character smiles.

Will your character have appropriate laugh lines? What about the eyes? Will an animator be able to create blinking and expressions easily with them?

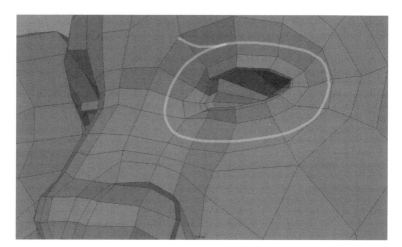

Figure 15-10: The eye edges are important for animation.

Here is the fish we created a while back. I know it's a little "Pixar-ish," but that's okay. You can already see the possibilities for expressions because I created the topology properly.

Figure 15-11: Proper topology for animation.

All the edge loops have a purpose on this model. You can see the edge loops that help form the laugh lines and cheeks. The fins come off the model using a series of edge loops, and the eyes are set up to blink and "express" properly.

Examples of Proper Edge Loops

I want to give you a few more examples of proper edge loops.
The following figures are from a work in progress.

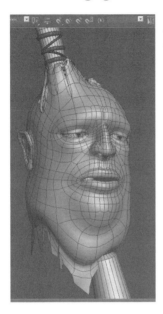

Figure 15-12:
Head on pole.

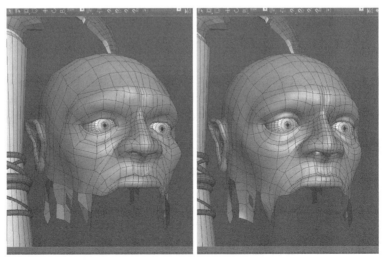

Figure 15-13: The image on the right is a smoothed version of the
image on the left.

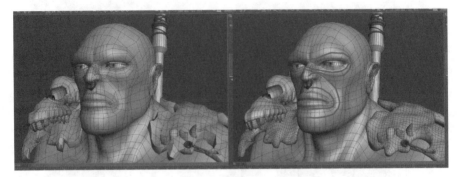

Figure 15-14: Another example of edge loops.

What is particularly interesting about these three characters is that they are all based on Figure 15-14. I modeled the character in Figure 15-14 first, and then simply modified the geometry to create the other two characters. The only reason I was able to do that is because I created the original character using good edge loops. This is another trick you will learn when creating things in production. You do not need to reinvent the wheel every single day. Why start a new head from scratch 184,734,728 times in a row? Create a good topology on your base character and then modify him to suit your needs. This will increase your workflow and ease the monotony of having to do the same thing over and over again. I work on teams all the time and my workflow is always faster than those around me. That is because I set up my workflow before I create anything. My hotkeys are set up for quick access, my interface is set up optimally, and I redo as little as possible. If that means reusing things or modifying existing art, then you need to do it. The artists did the same thing when making the characters for *The Incredibles*. Most of the secondary superheros as well as the background characters were just modifications of an original character. And from that one character they were able to move the polys around a bit and create men, women, children, tall characters, short characters, wide characters, and so on. This is a smart way to work. Start off smart and save time in the long term, not only for yourself, but for the others who may have to unwrap, paint, animate, or modify your model in the future.

The Realities of High-Poly Modeling

This section is just a short series of comments I'd like to make on the realities of high-poly modeling. First and foremost...(clearing throat)... Do not just TurboSmooth the hell out of your model and then think you've created a high-polygon model! If I see another person pick up a 3D application and make a 400,000-polygon character that would look the same if it were 6,000 polygons, I'm going to eat both of the wide-screen monitors I have in front of me!

Here is a pretty basic rule to follow: If you are adding polygons that do not add detail or information to one of your profiles (top, bottom, side), then you do not need those polygons.

Start off small when you get into your higher polygon models. You don't need to worry about the number; you need to worry about shape. You also need to be constantly looking at your model in its smoothed state. Sometimes you think you've got something really good going, then you apply the TurboSmooth modifier onto it and you lose a lot of detail. Or maybe you gain a lot of detail. Toggling back and forth should be part of your workflow. This will prevent you from having to go back and rework things.

The other thing you need to think about is what will actually be seen on camera. You certainly don't need to model something in great detail if it's going to be off in the distance and not a part of your focused shot. Oftentimes a really good animation or bit of texturing can completely trick the eye into believing what it's seeing. This is another aspect of improving your workflow. The goal is never to make the most complicated thing you can. CG elements are a fake. That's it. Your goal is to fool people into believing what they are seeing. Make creating the "fake" your goal, not creating the detail.

Setting Up Your Character Pose Properly

Most of this is common knowledge to anyone in the industry; however, if you are new to the game, this tip is important. When setting up your character, you need to have access to *all* of the character. What that means is, I need to be able to get to every nook and cranny of the character's body. I can't model the character's armpits if his arms are flat at his sides. I can't model inside the character's mouth if his mouth is completely closed, etc. You need your character to be standing upright in a "T" position.

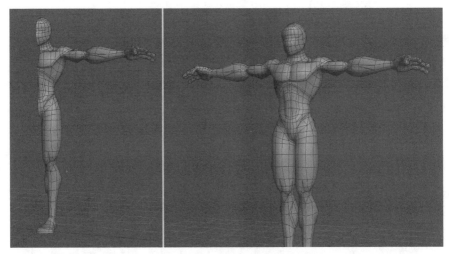

Figure 15-15: Model your character in the "T" position so you can access all sides.

You may get into some debates with people about the exact pose. Some may tell you that the full "T" position is the best, while others may want the arms bent a little at the shoulder and/or the elbows. All of these poses are great; the thing that is most important is that you are able to easily access all of your character. Leave it up to the animators to pose the character.

Breaking Down the Face into Parts

It's understandable if you find that creating a character's face is too daunting. It just means that we need to take a step back and look at the face in pieces. Don't overwhelm yourself by looking at the head as a whole. Break the face into parts and model them separately. Get good at modeling the nose. Open a scene and model a nose, next model an eye, then try a mouth, and so on. Get good at modeling all the things that make up a face. You can even merge all those pieces together in a final file to create a face.

Chapter 16

Using UVW Map and Unwrap UVW

What Does Unwrapping Mean?

Unwrapping is a term used to describe a part of the texturing process. Before you actually paint any textures you have to "unwrap" the object you want to texture. *Unwrapping* is the process of laying out your object's UVs in two dimensions in order to paint a texture over that layout. Think of it as taking something and flattening it like a pancake (although I'd much rather have a pancake than unwrap something).

 Note:

An object assigned to a 2D mapped material (or a material that contains 2D maps) must have mapping coordinates. These coordinates specify how the map is projected onto the material and whether it is projected as a "decal" or is tiled and mirrored. Mapping coordinates are also known as UV or UVW coordinates. These letters refer to coordinates in the object's own space as opposed to the XYZ coordinates that describe the scene as a whole.

Unwrapping an object has the potential to be a very time-consuming task. The more detail you have, the more time it will most likely take you to unwrap your object. Before I go any further, I'll show you an object and its corresponding unwrap.

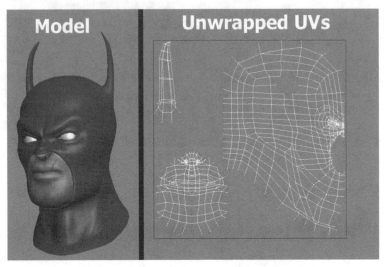

Figure 16-1: A model and the model after it is unwrapped.

It probably looks kind of weird to you, but this is what you see when you paint your textures. The unwrapped UVs are basically your canvas. You simply paint over the outlined area with the texture you desire. Just to be sure you know what you're looking at, I've made some notes to help you.

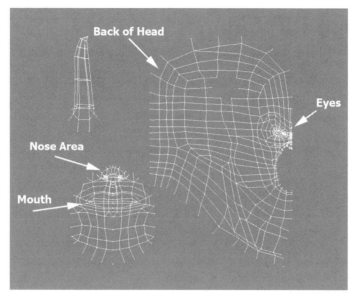

Figure 16-2: UV map.

What Is the Difference between UVW Map and Unwrap UVW?

There are two different modifiers that you'll be using in order to do your unwrapping: the UVW Map modifier and the Unwrap UVW modifier. "What's the difference?" you ask. Well, in short, the UVW Map modifier is the "quick and easy" way to unwrap something. It has presets and can drastically speed up the unwrapping process on very simple objects. The Unwrap UVW modifier is the manual way to unwrap an object. You'll use this on complex objects and objects where you need to control the exact UV layout. To better understand these, we'll go over them one at a time.

Using UVW Map

A UVW map is nothing more than a gizmo that will unwrap your object for you. How it unwraps your object is based on the gizmo of your choosing. You get seven basic presets when choosing your UVW map: Planar, Cylindrical, Spherical, Shrink Wrap, Box, Face, and XYZ to UVW. If you wish to unwrap a box, then of course you would want to choose the Box mapping. If you have a cylinder you wish you unwrap, then you would choose the Cylindrical mapping.

I'll demonstrate quickly just how the UVW Map modifier works. Let's create a cube within our Perspective viewport. The next thing we need is a material that will allow us to see how our unwrap is working. Open up your Material Editor and open the Maps rollout.

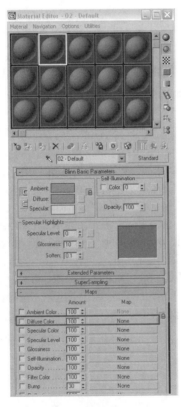

Figure 16-3:
Open the Maps
rollout.

The Maps rollout has several empty slots available. The second available slot is called the Diffuse Color channel. Diffuse Color is just a fancy way of saying color. You can load many different things into this slot, such as images, video, procedural textures, and so on. Click on the empty slot. This will bring up a very long list of options. Choose Checker.

Figure 16-4: Choose the Checker option for the Diffuse Color channel.

Checker is a procedural texture that is nothing more than a repeating checkered pattern. Such textures exist for this very purpose. Applying a checkered pattern onto your objects when you are unwrapping them provides you with a visual aid to keep your UVs straight and even. If your UVs are laid out improperly, then the checkered pattern will be flawed, as shown in Figure 16-5.

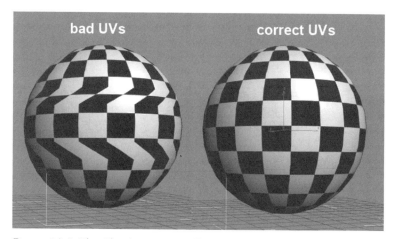

Figure 16-5: The Checker texture allows you to quickly see bad UVs.

Drag and drop your new material onto your cube. You may notice that nothing has happened, and your cube looks exactly the same. By default, materials do not show up in any 3D application because you don't always want to see your textures. Having your textures turned on will require more video card RAM, so being able to toggle these textures on and off as needed is very important. To toggle on and off your material, select the Checker material within the Material Editor.

Figure 16-6: Choose the Checker material.

The Checker material we are using should now be displayed.

 Note:

Any standard primitive will automatically generate its own UV coordinates. That is why our Checker material is showing up properly. Of course, if we were to modify the cube, then it would start to break down our UVs.

The Checker pattern looks good, but what if we wanted to modify our cube a bit? Let's adjust the width of the cube, which we know will stretch our UVs.

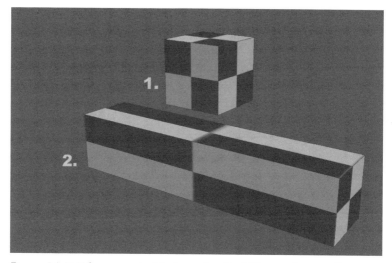

Figure 16-7: When you stretch the cube, the UVs stretch as well.

We want to fix our cube's mapping. It's the proper shape, but the UVs are obviously not even. This is where the UVW Map modifier comes in. Select your cube and apply the UVW Map modifier from your Modify panel. This will display a set of presets and options.

Figure 16-8: Applying the UVW Map modifier opens the Parameters rollout.

This is a pretty simple modifier that gives you a list of mapping options to choose from. Sometimes these options will totally solve your unwrap for you. Sometimes it will create a really good starting point. In this case we have a rectangle that we want to unwrap. A rectangle is basically a box, so let's choose the Box setting.

Figure 16-9: Choose the Box option from the Parameters rollout.

Now all that is necessary is to adjust the Width setting in the UVW Map modifier. Adjust the Width setting manually until you get the look you want. In this case we want the checkered pattern to be even. When you're done, the rectangle should look like this:

Figure 16-10: Adjust the Width setting until the checkered pattern is even.

It's perfect! It's beautiful! It's the most beautiful checkered rectangle in the whole of the universe!

 Note:

What is creating this new UV layout is the Box gizmo. That
gizmo is accessible on the sub-object level of your UVW
Map modifier. Like many other modifiers, notice that there
is a "+" symbol next to the UVW Map modifier. If you
open it up, you'll be able to access the Box gizmo.

Figure 16-11:
Click on the
"+" symbol to
access the Box
gizmo.

Once you highlight the Gizmo option, you'll notice a yellow
box appear in your Perspective viewport. This is your actual
gizmo. Now that you have access to the gizmo, take a minute
to see how it works. You can move, scale, and rotate the gizmo
to create different results.

Using the Unwrap UVW Modifier

We took the unwrapping process as far as we could using the
UVW Map modifier. If we wanted to up the level of control,
the next step would be to apply the Unwrap UVW modifier.
Something to keep in mind is that all 3D objects inherently
have UVs. The only way to actually see them, however, is to
apply the UVW Map modifier. Without the UVW Map modifier,
you cannot see or manually edit UVs.

The new Max 8.0 Unwrap UVW modifier is considerably
better than its previous versions, and it has gone almost
totally unnoticed by many. It's better for two reasons: the
addition of the Pelt mapping modifier, which I'll talk about a
little bit, and the added functionality of UVW Map into the
Unwrap UVW modifier. So technically you don't even need to

use the UVW Map modifier any more. This is actually pretty huge.

Let's select our handy checkered box and collapse it to an Editable Poly object. We no longer need anything in the history, so I like to start clean as often as possible. After you apply the modifier, you'll get a new list of options.

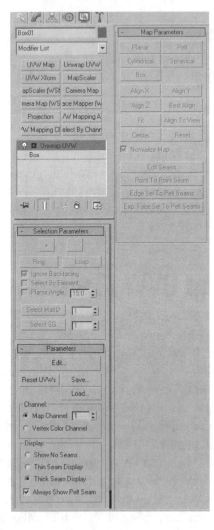

Figure 16-12: The Unwrap UVW Parameters rollout.

The bulk of your time will be spent using the options in the Parameters rollout of the modifier. Here you can do a couple of things, including edit, save, or load a set of UVs. Let's focus on the big one: editing UVs! Press the Edit button to get a whole new window with its own options.

Figure 16-13: Pressing the Edit button opens the Edit UVWs window.

I know that this window looks a bit complicated, but I can get you through the basics pretty quickly. First of all, let's get rid of that blue grid. If you are like me, it will give you a headache in under 15 minutes. So, choose the Options menu from the menu bar.

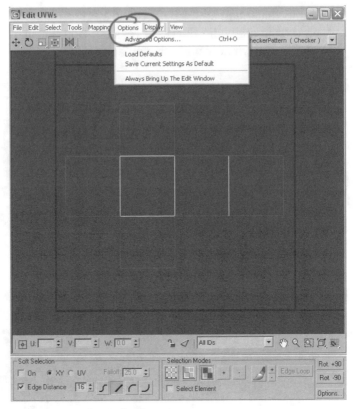

Figure 16-14: Open the Options menu.

Select Advanced Options, then uncheck the box labeled Show
Grid.

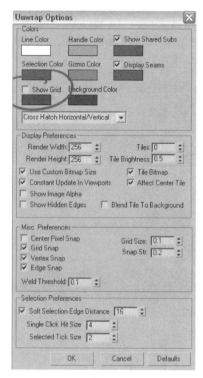

*Figure 16-15: The Unwrap Options
dialog.*

Of course you can keep the grid if you want, and you can even change the color so that you don't get a migraine. The dialog contains a number of other custom options for your Unwrap UVW modifier. Customize these settings to your liking. Once you have created a custom setup that you like, press the OK button at the bottom.

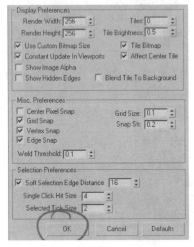

Figure 16-16: After choosing your custom settings, click OK.

Now go back to the Options menu and select Save Current
Settings As Default.

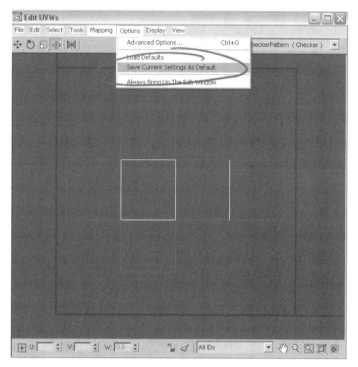

Figure 16-17: Save the new settings as the default.

This will ensure that the next time you access the modifier it
will display these custom settings.

Okay, on to the good stuff. I'll give you a quick rundown of
what most of this stuff means. At the top of the Edit UVWs
window you have the Move, Rotate, and Scale tools.

*Figure 16-18: The
Move, Rotate, and
Scale tools.*

Next to the Scale tool is the Freeform Mode tool.

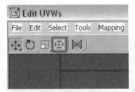

*Figure 16-19: The
Freeform Mode tool.*

This will allow you to modify any selected UVs using an adjustable box. Next to the Freeform Mode tool is the Mirror tool. You can mirror top to bottom or left to right.

*Figure 16-20: The
Mirror tool.*

To the right of the Mirror tool is a tool similar to the checkered cube that you have in the Material Editor. It serves the same purpose as the one in the Material Editor. Toggling this cube on and off will either display or turn off the texture you are using. This one, however, will not affect what is happening in your viewports; it only toggles the texture within your Edit UVW window.

Figure 16-21: The checkered cube toggles on and off the display of the material.

Note:

You also have right-click capabilities within your editing viewport to access tools such as Move, Rotate, and Scale. The right-click menu access can be quicker than going to the top of the editing window to access these options each time. At the bottom of the Edit UVWs window you'll notice another row of options.

Figure 16-22: At the bottom of the window are additional options.

You'll notice three empty boxes at the left: the U, V, and W positions. These are just like the X, Y, and Z positions in your 3D viewport. You can use these to type in exact positions for your UVs if necessary. To the right of that you'll see a triangle.

 Figure 16-23: Click the triangle button to display only selected faces.

The triangle is a toggle button that allows you to view selected faces only.

Just like the UVW Map modifier, the Unwrap UVW modifier has a sub-object level too. If you go back to the Unwrap UVW modifier and access its Face sub-object mode, you'll notice you can select the faces of your object.

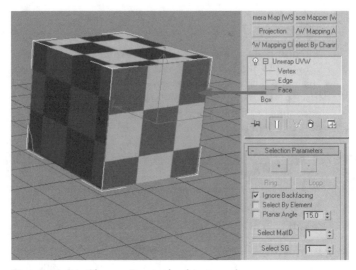

Figure 16-24: Choose Face sub-object mode.

If you have the triangle selected, then only the faces that are selected in your 3D viewport will show up in your Edit UVWs window.

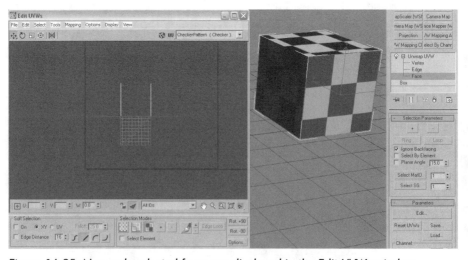

Figure 16-25: Now only selected faces are displayed in the Edit UVWs window.

This is a glorious feature, especially when dealing with complicated unwraps. Sometimes you don't want to see all the UVs and faces that you are not working on at that moment. Next to the triangle you have a material IDs drop-down.

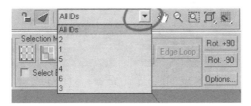

Figure 16-26: The Material IDs drop-down.

The drop-down will show you the available material IDs (if you have more than one). By default it will show you all material IDs.

To the right are the navigation tools, which are pretty self-explanatory. I recommend just using the mouse for all your navigation anyway; you can use the middle mouse wheel to move and zoom much faster.

On to the bigger stuff below the main editing viewport.

Figure 16-27: The Soft Selection and Selection Modes groups.

Most of these options are pretty self-explanatory also. You have Soft Selection options that work much the same as the Soft Selection options when editing polygon objects. You also have different selection modes, which by default is set to select UVs. You can select edges or faces, however, to speed up your workflow.

Next to the selection modes are the Grow and Shrink selection options. Again, this works just like the Grow and Shrink for your polygon objects. Most everything else in this box is pretty straightforward.

At the bottom right of the window is the Options button. Pressing this button reveals more options.

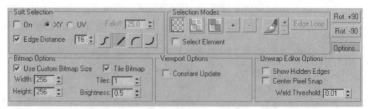

Figure 16-28: Press the Options button to see additional settings and check boxes.

These options are hidden because they are typically used less than the options above. With the bitmap and viewport options you can adjust the aspect ratio of your image, tile the image, adjust the brightness of the image, etc.

The last thing that I want to touch on is the Map Parameters rollout.

Figure 16-29: The Map Parameters rollout.

This is where all the improvements were made to Max 8.0's Unwrap modifier. Here you can now do planar, cylindrical, spherical, and box mapping all within the Unwrap UVW modifier instead of using the UVW Map modifier at all. You can also access the new Pelt unwrap (which is a massive upgrade).

Let's talk briefly about how all these new features work. First, let's note that the Map Parameters options work entirely at the sub-object level. Therefore, the rollout will be grayed out until you activate one of the sub-object modes of your Unwrap UVW modifier.

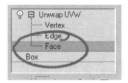

Figure 16-30: Activate a sub-object mode.

If we wanted to unwrap our trusty cube within the Map Parameters rollout, we would simply grab all the faces via our sub-object selection. Next, press the Box button in the Map Parameters rollout. Done! Just as before, if you want to see the unwrap or edit the vertices, you will have to open up the Edit UVWs window by pressing the Edit button in the Parameters rollout.

Figure 16-31: Press the Edit button on the Parameters rollout to open the Edit UVWs window.

This will also work with the cylindrical, spherical, and planer unwrap. Note that you can adjust the alignment of your unwrap to the X, Y, or Z axis. You can also align to view, fit, center, and best align your unwrap. Use these options on your own to see how they work. Practice unwrapping cylinders, boxes, and spheres using these new tools.

The last thing I want to talk about is the Pelt mapping modifier. This is an über tool. If you are just now getting into

3D, then you will not be able to appreciate this tool at all. If you've been in the business a while, then I'm sure you're just as excited as I am about this.

What is Pelt mapping? It's a mapping that stretches out all your UVs into a flat, unified surface, almost like it's a piece of cloth. To use the Pelt unwrap, you designate a series of seams and then tell Max to unwrap it for you. This is intended to work on organic objects that would normally be very tedious or difficult to do.

I've got a head set up that I'll unwrap really quick. Normally, this could take an hour or more. I can do it in about two or three minutes now with the Pelt modifier.

To use the Pelt map modifier we just need to designate the seams. To do this, we need to select all the faces on our object so we can see the seams, which should be highlighted in blue. In this example it should be done for us, as Max designates any open edge as a Pelt seam by default.

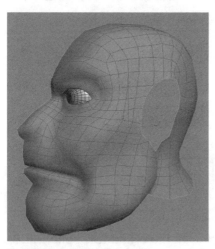

Figure 16-32: The seams are highlighted in blue.

So actually with this model we don't need to make any adjustments. However, if this were a closed model, we would have to designate the seams. You can do this very easily using the

Point To Point Seam option. If, for example, I wanted to make another seam across our character's face, I would activate the Point To Point Seam option.

Figure 16-33: Choose Point To Point Seam to add a seam.

Next, just select one vertex for the beginning of the seam and another for the end of the seam.

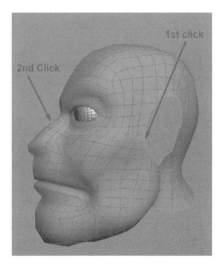

Figure 16-34: Click on two vertices where you want the seam.

We don't actually want to keep that middle seam, so you can get rid of it by selecting the Edit Seams option. Holding Alt and reselecting the seam will get rid of it.

Now press the Pelt button located in the Map Parameters rollout.

Figure 16-35:
Press the Pelt
button.

Just as before when we used the Map Parameters options, we now have to select an axis to perform our Pelt on. Most of the time, Best Align will work the best. Choose Best Align, and Max will display something like the following for you.

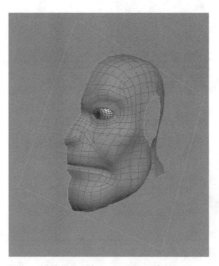

Figure 16-36: Choose Best Align.

Now that the angle is selected, all that is left to do is perform the Pelt action. Select Edit Pelt Map located at the bottom of your Map Parameters rollout.

Figure 16-37:
Click on Edit
Pelt Map.

This opens the Pelt Map Parameters dialog and a new editing window.

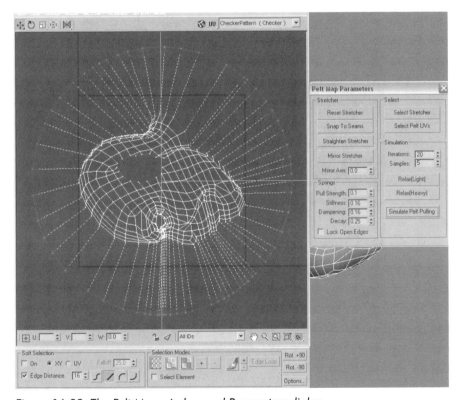

Figure 16-38: The Pelt Map window and Parameters dialog.

I'll just explain briefly what is going on here. In the window to the left you have your unwrap. The circle with the lines is your "stretcher." The stretcher pulls and stretches your UVs flat, like a piece of cloth. To the right is the Pelt Map Parameters dialog box. The only two buttons we will use for this map are the Simulate Pelt Pulling and the Relax(Light) buttons. So even though it looks like a lot, we're really only doing a couple of things.

Now we need to give our stretcher room to operate, so active your Scale tool and scale up the stretcher.

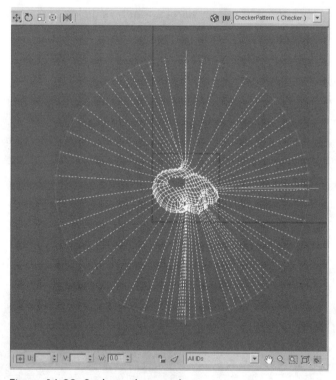

Figure 16-39: Scale up the stretcher.

This will give our stretcher a little more room to work. Now press the Simulate Pelt Pulling button.

Figure 16-40: Press the Simulate Pelt Pulling button.

Your UVs should get pulled out like this:

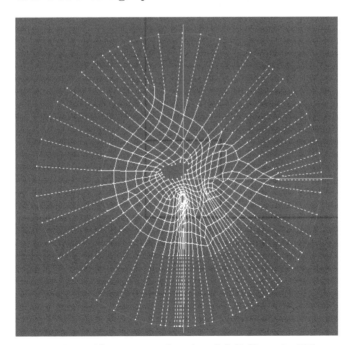

Figure 16-41: After pressing Simulate Pelt Pulling, the UVs look like this.

You can still see that it's a little too "busy" in the middle, so let's do one more Simulate Pelt Pull on this guy. Press the button again and it'll smooth the UVs out a little more. Now it's looking pretty good. If you are looking at your model with the checkered pattern at this point, it looks pretty good, but there are a few areas where it's a bit warped.

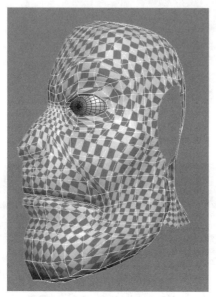

Figure 16-42: A few areas of the model need some adjustment.

To fix this, just press the Relax(Light) button several times until you get the results you want. It may take several clicks, but when you are done it should look pretty nice.

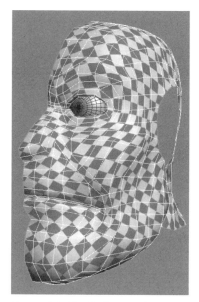

*Figure 16-43: Clicking Relax
(Light) a few times fixes the
warped areas.*

When you are done, make sure you're still in Face sub-object
mode, go back up to the Map Parameters rollout, and press
the Pelt button. Now you will be able to manually edit any
remaining UVs that you are unhappy with.

Chapter 17

Advanced Modeling Exercise: The Human Ear

I have some good news and some bad news. The good news is that you are going to learn how to model the human ear. The bad news is that we have to model a human ear! Arrrrgggg! I love modeling, as anyone will tell you. Modeling an ear, however, isn't exactly the most fun thing on the planet. It's damn near impossible to do if you don't know where to start. Although there are many ways to create an ear, over the years I've adopted a certain way of doing it. I didn't come up with the idea or anything, but it's the best technique that I've seen.

I'd also like to give you a sweet piece of advice: Model an ear *once*. Make the best ear you possibly can. Spend a year on it if you have to. When you are done, you don't ever have to do it again. There is no reason for you to model a set of ears on every character you ever make. Even if you have very specific ears, the one that we make in this chapter will be the base for all of them. You can always modify the existing model. I suppose there are times when you may want to make one from scratch, but it's always better to work smart and not hard.

Before you just go diving into making an ear, you need to take a close, hard look at how the ear is put together. It's a pretty organic and fluid piece of hardware. But you only really need to focus on a few main areas in order to get it looking like an ear.

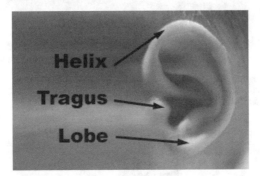

Figure 17-1: The main areas of the ear to focus on.

You definitely need to get the helix of the ear looking right. It should be folded over at the top and thicker as it gets closer to the opening of the ear. The tragus should be sticking out off the side of the head a bit from where it connects the ear to the head. And of course we all know about the lobe. If you can nail these three basic shapes, you should have a pretty convincing-looking ear.

I'm going to quickly outline for you how we are going to start the ear. For the most part, the ear has one basic shape happening. It's a path that starts from the tragus and goes all the way up and around the back of the ear down to the earlobe.

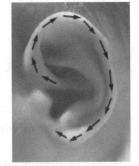

Figure 17-2: The ear's path starts at the tragus and continues clockwise to the earlobe.

Since the outer edge is the base for the entire shape of the ear, we are going to start here first. I always recommend using a reference image if you need it (see ear ref.jpg in the downloadable files). If not, you can certainly freehand it like I'm going to do.

Here we go! We are basically going to manually loft the shape of the ear. You want to start off with a cube in your Perspective viewport. Then begin the shaping of the ear.

Figure 17-3: Start the tragus as a cube, then start adding the helix.

This is the perfect start. You may be wondering what we just made. Here is a picture to help you understand.

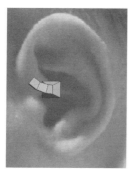

Figure 17-4: The reference picture is in the background.

From here we are going to continue this path all the way around the ear.

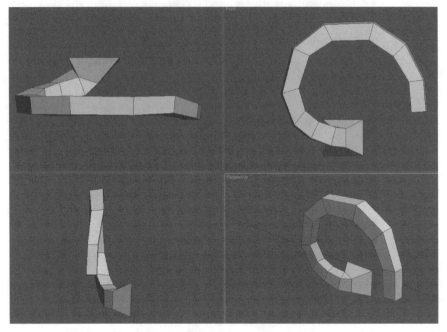

Figure 17-5: Continue adding segments around the helix.

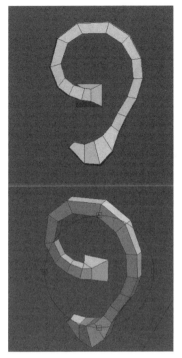

Figure 17-6: Add the earlobe last.

Once you get all the way around the basic ear shape, it should actually look a bit like a question mark. The next move will be to make the connection from the earlobe back up to the helix. You can do this manually. You can also use the Bridge tool. Select the two corresponding faces and delete them, then grab the open edges using the Border button. Finally, apply the Bridge tool. You will find it in the Edit Borders rollout in the Modify panel.

Figure 17-7: Select the open edges using the Border button.

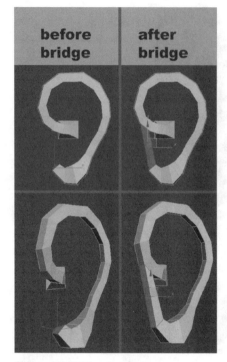

Figure 17-8: Here's what your ear should look like.

You can actually use the Bridge tool to add segments to your bridge. We will need to add a few segments in order to tweak the bridge a bit.

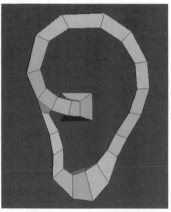

Figure 17-9: Add a few segments with the Bridge tool.

Well, that's about it. This is our basic ear shape. It is still a box, however, so we are going to have to start smoothing it out. I'd like to add an edge loop all the way around the ear and pull it out slightly. This will start to give our ear more of a realistic tube shape.

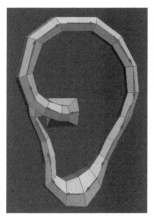

Figure 17-10: Smooth, then add an edge loop and pull it out slightly.

Repeat that same process along the back side of the ear as well. You can't leave the back side of the ear flat, of course.

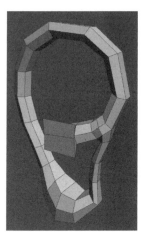

Figure 17-11: Repeat the process for the back side of the ear.

Before we cap the inside of the ear and begin creating detail, we need to delete the polygons on the back side of the ear. This will allow us to create the rear connection for the ear. It also allows us to cap the inside in the next step. Delete the polygons that are selected in the left side of Figure 17-12. Then select the open border and Shift+scale it down.

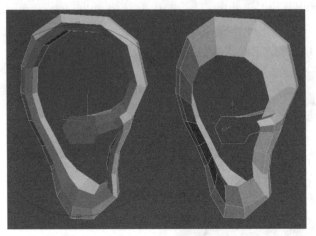

Figure 17-12: Delete the selected polygons, then select the open border and Shift+scale it down.

For now this will complete the back side of the ear. Now we can move on to the fun part: all the organic curves and twists of the inner ear! (The crowd cheers.) To do this, you will need to select the open border in the front of the ear and "cap" it. You'll find the Cap function in the lower-left quad of your right-click menu. You can also find it in the Modify panel under the Edit Borders rollout. All capping does is create a cap with no edges, so the cap may look a bit confusing. The idea is that we'll create the cap and then manually add the edges.

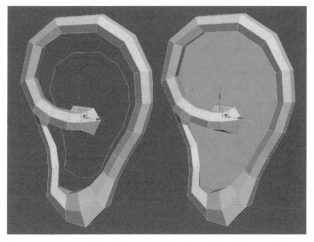

Figure 17-13: Select the open border of the front of the ear and cap it.

The next part is very important. You want to start making connections, but you need to do so logically. The modeling process for the ear is very organic. You may create a bunch of edges, and then as you progress you may make changes in order to clean up your edge loops. In the end, if your edge loops are different from mine, that's fine. The important thing is that you created them with some sort of logic. First off, I just want to make some basic connections.

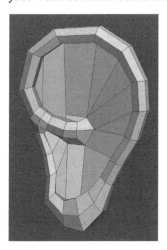

Figure 17-14: Create some basic connections.

You may start to feel like I am jumping ahead in larger steps from here on out, which is true. I won't articulate every single cut for you, but rather provide you with a guide and a technique to creating the ear.

Next, you want to start creating your edge loops that will create the detail in the ear. Naturally, you don't want them to be going up and down. You want to follow the original shape of the ear that we created.

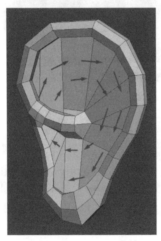

Figure 17-15: Start creating edge loops that follow the original shape.

I am going to quickly start adding some edge loops with this direction in mind.

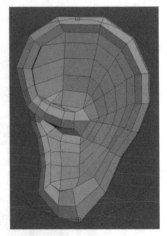

Figure 17-16: The added edge loops.

You can really start to see already how easy it will be to push in and pull out the appropriate areas with these edge loops set up the way they are. At this point, all we really need to do is start to push and pull certain parts of the edge loops.

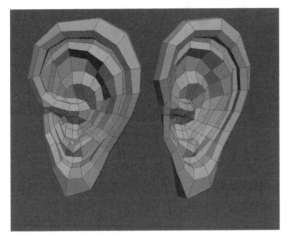

Figure 17-17: Create the inner ear shapes with the new edge loops.

When doing this, you really need to refer to your reference photo a lot. One of the biggest problems people have when creating human ears is that they just start making things up. They will pull out areas that don't exist in the real world. Pay attention to your reference photos and really try to mimic the parts that are going in and the parts that are going out. You can also tell that I have been making changes to the overall shape of the ear as I go. If you look at someone's ear when you are face to face, it is not perfectly vertical. It bends outward a bit and has some curve to it.

Believe it or not, at this point you are actually pretty much good to go. We are missing a couple of small details, however. Let's add them now and be done! We need to create the ear hole. For this we just need to grab polys in the proper area and bevel them inward. Don't just punch a hole in our guy's ear, either. Make sure that the hole is facing the proper direction. The hole doesn't go straight into the head; it actually faces away from the face. You will most likely want to bevel it inward a couple of times in order to get it looking right.

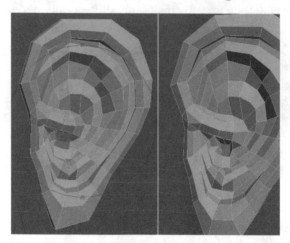

Figure 17-18: Create the ear hole.

After you get that looking sexy, you want to make sure you have the tragus (what I call the hole "cover"). It just protects the actual opening a bit.

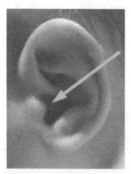

Figure 17-19: The tragus (or hole "cover").

This one is easy too. Just find the two corresponding polygons and extrude them outward. That should act as a good enough "cover."

Figure 17-20: Create the tragus.

I'd say we are done. Of course, you can continue moving edges forward a bit to create some of the surrounding skin that will attach the ear to the head. When you are done with the whole thing, it should be pretty close to what looks like a convincing ear.

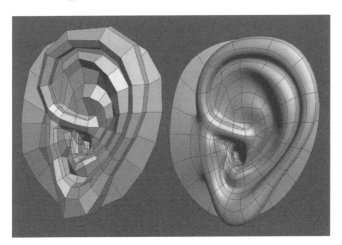

Figure 17-21: The completed ear.

Chapter 18

Animation Basics

Animation! Wow, where to begin? First, let me get a few
things out of the way. Animation is a very difficult and very
specialized skill. In fact, within the professional world of 3D,
animation is something that you either "do" or "do not."
There are few 3D artists who are also animators, and there
are few animators who are 3D artists. Being a professional
animator requires full-time dedication, which is not uncommon in the professional world. Similarly, few compositors are
animators, and most 3D artists are not Avid editors. Now don't
get me wrong; there are many artists out there who can do
some of everything, but when you get down to it, the character animators at Pixar are not doing environmental modeling
in between their animation schedule. There are specialized
animation teams, modeling teams, compositors, editors, and
so on.

The reality is, if you want to become an animator, then you
should run right out and purchase a book on animation. Even
if I wrote 100 pages on animation, I would not have scratched
the surface. All I intend to do in this chapter is show you a few
basic principles of animation to dip your little toe into the pool
that is animation.

Creating and Deleting Keys

Animation is created by setting keys. A *key* is simply a point in time that retains specific information. It can store time data, rotation values, position information, and so on.

Let's do something simple to show you the basics. Create a sphere in your Perspective viewport. We want to animate the sphere moving horizontally across the viewport. To do that, we first need to activate the Auto Key button located at the bottom right of your user interface.

Figure 18-1: Activate the Auto Key button.

The Auto Key button is like the Record button on your VCR. All movement, rotation, and scale changes are keyframed while the Auto Key button is activated. After you press the Auto Key button, it should be highlighted in red.

Figure 18-2: When activated, the Auto Key button is highlighted in red.

In order to create an animation, we need to designate a "time" and an "action." The "action" is the actual animated event. The "time" is obviously at what frame you want that action to occur. Here are a few background basics: When you are animating, you will normally animate at 30 frames per second. That means you are taking 30 pictures each second. If you are animating for film, however, you will animate at 24 frames per second. (But since you bought the *Essentials* book, it's pretty likely that you're not doing film animation!)

Let's set the time first. Let's say we want our ball to move horizontally across the Perspective viewport in one second. That means we need to move our time slider to frame 30. The time slider shows you the current frame. It also lets you move to any frame in your active time segment.

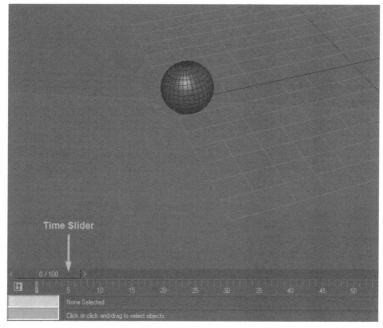

Figure 18-3: The time slider.

Make sure that you still have Auto Key turned on, and then manually move the time slider to frame 30.

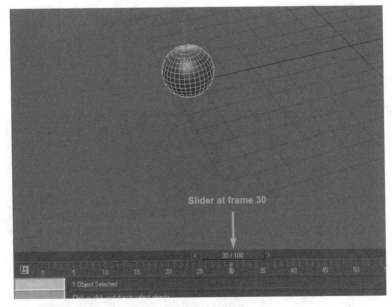

Figure 18-4: Move the time slider to frame 30.

Now take the sphere and move it across the screen on the X axis. You'll notice that if you look at the time slider, two keyframes have been created — a key at 0.0, which represents the starting point, and a key at frame 30.

To view your animation you can manually move the slider to frame 0 again. Just mouse over it and drag it back and forth from 0 to 30. This is very helpful when you are viewing your animations. You'll also note that you have playback controls at the bottom right of the UI.

Figure 18-5: The playback controls.

The playback controls are pretty obvious. You can play, stop, go frame by frame forward and backward, and so on. You also have a button that opens up the Time Configuration dialog box.

Figure 18-6: The Time Configuration button.

Pressing this will open up a new dialog.

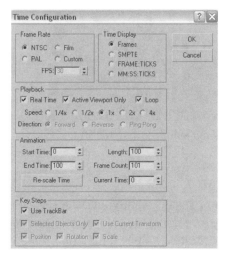

Figure 18-7: The Time Configuration dialog.

Most of the options in this dialog are pretty self-explanatory. As I explained before, you can adjust your frame rate in the Frame Rate options group in the upper-left corner. You can choose from NTSC, which is the default 30 FPS setting; Film, which is 24 frames per second; or PAL, which runs at 25 frames per second. You can also choose a custom number of frames per second. You'll never want to change this from its default setting unless you are doing film, as I mentioned before.

You can adjust your playback speed very quickly with the Playback settings. There are five options: 1/4x, 1/2x, 1x, 2x, and 4x. You can also choose whether or not to have your animations loop. By default, Loop is checked. That means when your time slider gets to the end of the active time segment, it will start over at frame 0 and play again.

The settings you'll use the most, however, are the Animation settings. Here you can adjust your time segment's start time and end time. By default, the length of your active time segment is 100 frames.

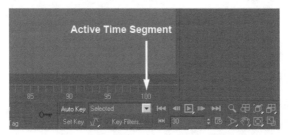

Figure 18-8: The default length of time is 100 frames.

Obviously, you don't always want your time segment to end at frame 100. You may be doing work for game in which you only have 60 frames to create a looping animation. Likewise, you may need to do a single animation shot that requires thousands of frames of animation. So you'll be adjusting the Animation settings often in your animation career.

Okay, let's get back to our ball! Right now our animated ball is traveling only on the X axis. Let's add more movement to our animation. Move your time slider to frame 15 and move the ball up on the Z axis to your desired height. Now watch your animation again. The ball should be traveling up and down while it moves to the right.

Figure 18-9: Add vertical movement to the animation.

Note the timeline at the bottom of the UI displays your keys for you. You can move these keys within your timeline by dragging them to the desired time. You can also right-click these keys to reveal more options.

Almost anything in Max is animateable. We can animate the actual radius of the sphere also. Drag the time slider to frame 15 and change the radius of the sphere to be much smaller. Now move the time slider to frame 30 and change the radius to be larger again. Now the sphere is traveling up and down and left to right with the radius of the sphere changing also.

This is obviously a very simple example of animation; however, this layering we're doing is a normal way to build up your animations. You start out with the basic positions at desired time frames (called *blocking*) and then you add the in-betweens and details.

There are a few ways to adjust existing keyframes. You can do very basic adjustments within the main UI just by right-clicking a keyframe. For example, if you right-click on the keyframe located at frame 30, you'll get a small list of options.

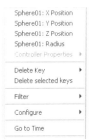

Figure 18-10: Right-click on a keyframe to display a menu of options.

You'll see X, Y, and Z position information, as well as the radius that we animated. If, for example, you wanted to adjust the radius, you'd select Sphere01: Radius. This would bring up another dialog that would allow you to make adjustments to the sphere's radius as well as its time.

Figure 18-11:
Choose Sphere01:
Radius to display
this dialog.

When it comes time for you to take your animating to the next level and you need to start making real adjustments to your animations, you'll need to start using the Curve Editor. The Curve Editor displays your animation as function curves. Function curves give you the ability to really tweak your animations. To open up the Curve Editor, press the Curve Editor button located at the top right of your UI.

Figure 18-12: The Curve Editor button.

The Curve Editor is a fairly complicated tool that is beyond the scope of this book. If you want to learn the Curve Editor inside and out I suggest taking a look at the reference files that 3ds Max provides. You can also explore it yourself, or pick up a book that focuses on animation specifically.

Chapter 19

Creating a Basic Composite over a Background Plate

For this final chapter we're going to create a composite inside of Max. I'm also going to show you how to create a matte so that your two-dimensional image can receive shadows as if it's a real three-dimensional world. Figures 19-1 and 19-2 are some examples of images that I created outside of my office. Everything in these shots was modeled, lit, and composited inside of 3D Studio MAX.

Figure 19-1

Figure 19-2

Now in the real world of visual FX, compositing is very serious craft. These guys are nothing short of miracle workers. They are the ones who put everything together, including shadows, clouds, blood, explosions, characters, background plates, foreground plates, and so on. All these things need to be placed in a single frame and look 100 percent convincing. The best example of this ever put on film in my opinion is *The Lord of the Rings*. Obviously that composite work was not done within a 3D package like we are about to do. Their work is entirely too complicated, not to mention all the camera tracking involved. They no doubt used massive Avid editing suites with very, very talented artists and editors at the controls.

This is not *The Lord of the Rings*, however! All I am going to show you is the absolute essentials. We are going to load up a background plate and place a cube or standard primitive within the scene. Then I'll show you how to create a matte on the ground so the cube can cast a shadow onto the 2D image.

Loading Your Background Image

Before we begin you'll need to load up the background image that we'll be using. There are two different things you must take into consideration when setting this up. You want to make sure that when you render the scene, Max will render the background image we assign as the background. Also, you will want to make sure that you can see the background image inside your camera viewport. First, we'll make sure our background is renderable, then we'll load it into our camera viewport.

From the main menu, select Rendering>Environment.

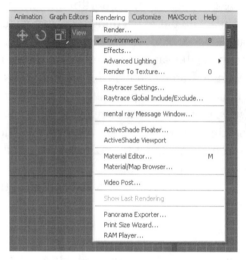

Figure 19-3: Choose Environment from the Rendering menu.

This will open the Environment and Effects dialog box, which has several options.

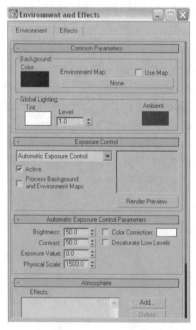

Figure 19-4: The Environment and Effects dialog.

The only portion of this dialog that we will need to worry about is the Environment Map setting. You'll notice an empty slot just below, labeled None. This is where we will load our background image from the companion files: image_5.jpg. When you are done, your Environment Map slot should look like this:

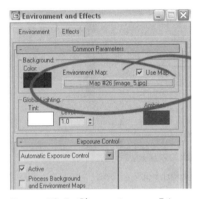

Figure 19-5: Choose image_5.jpg from the companion files for the background image.

Don't forget to check the Use Map check box. This check box acts as a toggle button. There may be times when you don't want to see the background image when you render. If you don't, then simply uncheck this box. Now that we have the Environment and Effects settings correctly configured, our background will show up when we render. We just need to view this background in our viewport. From the main menu, choose Views>Viewport Background to open the Viewport Background dialog.

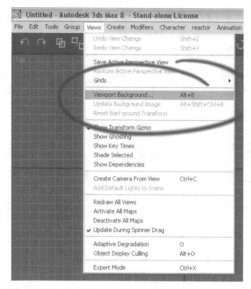

Figure 19-6: Choose Viewport Background from the Views menu.

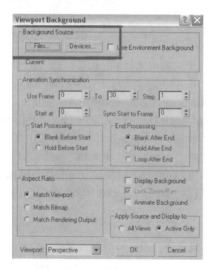

Figure 19-7: The Viewport Background dialog.

In the Background Source group, choose the Files button to load the same background image that we loaded before. You can also just check the Use Environment Background check box. That tells Max that we want to use the same image as in the rendered background we set up just a second ago. Either way is fine. Once you are done, you should see a glorious background appear in your Perspective viewport.

Figure 19-8: The background image in the Perspective viewport.

You may or may not notice that the background image is a bit blurry, depending on your personal settings. By default, Max will use a slightly compressed version of the image in order to save video memory. Our scene is not very big, so you may want to adjust those settings, which are located in Customize > Preferences… > Viewports > Configure Driver. Just check the box that is labeled Match Bitmap as Closely as Possible to tell Max to use the same size image as the original photograph. If you were working in film, you might have images that are something like 4 gigapixels. Yeah, I said gigapixels. Even trying to use something drastically smaller could be problematic. So you have the option of letting Max view that image at different default sizes.

Now let's talk about a few boring details. There are a few things to think about and set up in advance when you are doing a composite shot. First of all, you need to know your camera aspect ratio. Will it be 16:9 or a custom setting? In this case we know that the image we are using is 2592 x 1944. (This is a totally bizarre size, but it's what my camera took, so that's the aspect ratio we will use.) Open up your render options and change the default 640 x 480 width and height to 2592 x 1944. This ensures that you won't crop any of your background when you render.

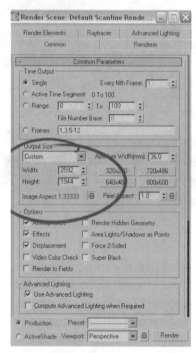

Figure 19-9: Set the width and height to 2592 x 1944.

To see your actual clipping planes within your viewport, you need to right-click on the word Perspective in your viewport and check Show Safe Frame. This will border your shot for you.

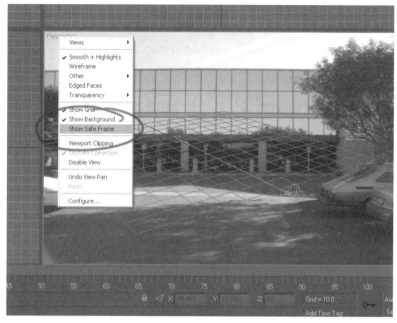

Figure 19-10: Right-click the Perspective label and choose Show Safe Frame.

Figure 19-11: Now the Perspective viewport displays clipping planes.

You can see how Max has pulled in the image horizontally. It's now being displayed properly in your viewport. It was actually stretching to fit the viewport before.

Adding a Ground Plane with a Matte Material to Match the Environment

Now that we have our background image loaded and ready to render, we need to add a three-dimensional ground plane and line it up with our scene. This ground plane will serve a couple of purposes. It will give us a guide to line up our perspective from the 2D photo to the 3D object, and it will also receive the shadow when we light our scene. This is very important because the shadow is what will actually put the object within the photograph.

Create a plane in the Perspective viewport.

Figure 19-12: Create a plane in the Perspective viewport.

When you create the plane it will no doubt come in at a different angle than our background photo. I like to have plenty of length and width segments in my plane because I feel like it's easier to line things up this way. It gives me more reference points. Also, I specifically chose this background picture because of the windows in the building in the background. These give me something very easy to align my ground plane to.

Use your viewport navigation controls to position the plane in front of the windows. (Don't use the Move and Rotate controls; instead, use the Perspective viewport navigation controls: Zoom, Pan, Rotate view, etc.) Line up the window borders with your plane border.

Figure 19-13: Line up the plane with the windows in the background.

This should give us a pretty good starting point. Now, using your navigation controls, move the plane straight down. Use any part of the scene as reference. Notice a slight color change in the asphalt just below the handicap parking area. I used this as a marker to drop down my ground plane.

Figure 19-14: Move the plane down below the handicap parking area.

This is going to be about perfect for what we are doing. If you can't quite find the right perspective in a scene, you may try adding a cube on the ground plane to align other parts of the scene.

 Note:

The human eye basically looks at things with a 45-degree field of view. If your background scene or movie footage is using something other than a 45-degree angle, then your objects will never align to your view. It's just impossible. Don't worry, however, if you are using wacky camera angles and different tricks; then you probably know what you're doing.

Now that we have our ground plane lined up, we'll need to apply a matte material to it. The matte material is a material that will render invisible except for things cast onto it or bouncing off of it (shadows or reflections). Open up your Material Editor and press the Standard button. This will open up your Material/Map Browser. The Material/Map Browser has several default materials. We want to select the Matte/Shadow material.

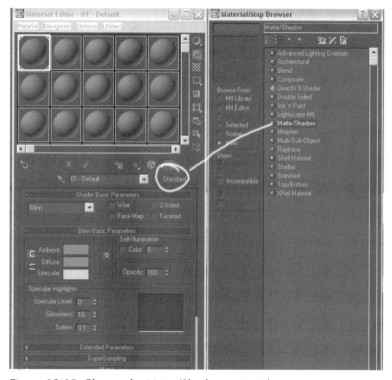

Figure 19-15: Choose the Matte/Shadow material.

After you load the Matte/Shadow material, you'll notice your Material Editor shows several new options. By default you should not need to do anything. The matte should be set to receive shadows and also affect the alpha. If the Receive Shadows and Affect Alpha boxes are not already checked, then make sure they are checked.

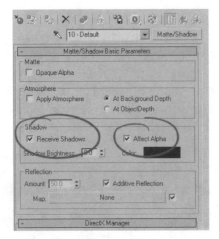

*Figure 19-16: Be sure the Receive
Shadows and Affect Alpha check
boxes are checked.*

Lighting and Rendering Your Scene

Now that we have our matte shadow, we need to create some
kind of lighting for our scene. But before we do that, we need
to place an object onto our ground plane. This will give our
lights something to hit, and therefore cast shadows. I'm going
to use a torus, which you can find in the Extended Primitives
rollout. I'm going to place it into the scene at the appropriate
size. I'm also going to increase the size of our ground plane. I
need to make sure any shadows cast don't fall off the edge, so
I'll just increase it to be sure.

Figure 19-17: Place a torus on the ground plane and enlarge the plane so that shadows won't fall off the edge.

Because this is an outdoor shot, I usually use a two-light setup. You definitely need a direct light source (the sun), and then an ambient light source to prevent the areas in shadow from being completely black. Let's create the ambient light source first. You can do this manually or you can use Max's skylight. The skylight is one of Max's most powerful features and I recommend that you use it as often as you can. Just don't use it as your *only* means of lighting. Create a skylight in your scene. Figure 19-18 shows the settings I'm using for my skylight.

Figure 19-18: The skylight settings.

Make sure the skylight is turned on. You may also want to adjust your light color to match your scene. You can even get very crazy with this thing and load HDR lights and other stuff to match your lighting via the photo, but we're keeping this simple for now. I am going to use a blue color for the ambient lighting in this case. By default, your shadow sample is 20. I change mine to 10 just to speed up render tests. When you final your shot, you'll up this number again to the desired number. The Multiplier setting is how intense your light is. We may adjust this up or down depending on how this scene starts turning out. Let's go ahead and do a test render with these settings.

Figure 19-19: Our first render.

Ha, I'm getting pretty good at guessing these settings, I guess. That actually looks pretty good. Oh, and before I forget, I need to mention something about the render size. Like I said earlier in this chapter, the background picture size is 2592 x 1944. That doesn't mean you need to render at this size; it just means you need to keep that aspect ratio. To lock down this aspect ratio, simply press the Lock icon in your render settings.

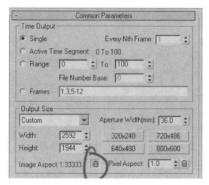

Figure 19-20: Press the Lock icon to maintain the aspect ratio.

You can now freely change the size of your render to your heart's content and Max will maintain this aspect ratio for you. That way you can lower your render size to something realistic and not kill your render times.

Okay, with that said, let's create our sunlight. Normally I'd tell you to use a light with a raytrace shadow. Oftentimes the sunlight is a very direct source and casts a pretty crisp shadow. But in this shot you have to use your shadows as a reference and try to match them. The shadows we have in front of the torus are pretty blurry, actually. They are also a bit blue. And they are not just solid black shadows. These are things to keep in mind when matching the lighting by hand.

Let's just use a basic spotlight. Be sure to cast your light in the same direction as the sun. In this case, it's coming from the front left of our scene.

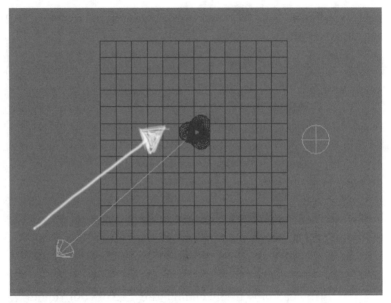

Figure 19-21: The position of the spotlight.

Mess around with the spotlight yourself to see what you can come up with. I kept most of the light's defaults actually, but I did make a few minor adjustments. I have Multiplier set to .7 and my shadow density set to 1.5 instead of the default 1.0. Make sure your hotspot and falloff are encompassing the entire scene. If you render your scene with similar settings, you should get something like Figure 19-22.

Figure 19-22: The final render.

You can take compositing as far as your mind can wander. If we were doing this for real, you may start thinking about the torus reflecting things in its environment, or perhaps the wall of windows has the torus in its reflection. You may want to cast a fake shadow across the torus, as if the tree next to it is putting it partly in shadow because of its leaves. You can even start playing around with HDR lighting at this point and create your own HDR images. We are literally at the most basic stages here, but you get the "essentials" at this point!

Index

time slider, 41-42
toolbars,
    creating, 26-30
    docking, 26
torso,
    adding detail to, 232-233, 235-236
    creating, 230-232
triangles, avoiding, 87
TurboSmooth,
    stacking, 226-228
    using, 186-189
    vs. MeshSmooth, 224-225
Twist modifier, using, 184-185

U
Unwrap Options dialog, 343-344
Unwrap UVW modifier, 333
    using, 339-359
Unwrap UVW Parameters rollout,
    340-341
unwrapping, 331-333
user interface, 13
    customizing, 22-30
    customizing colors in, 42-43
    tearing off parts of, 24-25
user interface layout,
    loading custom, 30
    saving, 30
UV coordinates, 331
UVW coordinates, 331
UVW map, 334
UVW Map modifier, 333
    using, 334-339

V
vertex weighting, 191
vertices,
    chamfering, 109
    changing corner type for, 176
    connecting, 103
    inserting, 104
    selecting, 80-81
Vertices button, 80
view, bringing object into, 17
Viewport Background dialog, 388-389
Viewport Configuration dialog, 20-21
viewport handles, adjusting, 61
viewport layout, modifying, 18-21
viewport navigation tools, 14
viewports, 14
    maximizing, 15
    panning in, 15-16
    rotating in, 16
    zooming in, 14-15

W
walls,
    adding detail to, 207-213
    creating, 199-203
windows, adding to floor plan, 206-207
window primitives, 6

X
XYZ coordinates, 2

Z
Zoom Extents tool, 17
Zoom tool, 14-15